Worthy of the Jersey:

An exhilarating journey of a high school basketball program, its head coach, and a special championship season

by

Norm Weber

with Eric Flannery

Illustrations by St. Edward High School unless otherwise noted

Student/Athlete-Cleveland Publishing
Design, Production and Printing by Kaptur Design
Cover Concept and Photography by K.C. McKenna

Table of Contents

Table of Contents v
Acknowledgements vii
Forward ix
Introduction xi
Chapter One – Earned, not Given 1
Chapter Two – Worthy of the Jersey, Big Mike 9
Chapter Three – Jumping Out to an Eye-Opening Start 17
Chapter Four – Mind Candy, Toughness and The Fist 35
Chapter Five – The Holy Cross Philosophy 47
Chapter Six – Worthiness Means No. 18 Counts as Much as No. 1 51
Chapter Seven – Worthy of the Winning Streak 61
Chapter Eight – Worthiness in Offseason Preparation 71
Chapter Nine – Last Play History, Next Play Now 79
Chapter Ten – Losing With Dignity a Worthy Act 85
Chapter Eleven – Learning Goes with Earning 93
Chapter Twelve – Flan's History as a Worthy Edsman 99
Chapter Thirteen – Flannery and USA Basketball 119
Chapter Fourteen – Being Worthy of the Family 125
Chapter Fifteen – Worthy of Staying or Leaving 137
Chapter Sixteen – Power Shift 145
Chapter Seventeen – At St. Ed's, Success Breeds Success 151
Chapter Eighteen – St. Ed's Basketball Greatness in the '90s, '00s, '10s 155
Chapter Nineteen – Less Talent but Better Results 161
Chapter Twenty – Getting Worthier During Tournament Clean-up Time 169
Chapter Twenty-One – The Final Goal Accomplished and Truly Worthy of the Jersey 183
Epilogue – Worthy of the Next Play, Continuing the Tradition 199
Bibliography 204

Acknowledgements

During the research phase of this production the data to compile the book had to be collected, which would not have been possible with all the individuals who granted live interviews. For these interviews, thanks go to Lori Flannery, Coach Eric Flannery, Pat Riley, Tony Vuyancih, Malcolm Walters, Kipper Nichols, Marsalis "Sal" Hamilton, Phil Parente, Connor Pisco, and Coaches Delvon Blanton, Josh Nugent, Danny Gallagher, T.J. Gallagher, Brian Ansberry, and Tom Bodle.

We would also like to thank all 18 student-athletes on the team who contributed their Worthy-of-the-Jersey essays. Among those who contributed were Riley, Vuyancih, Walters, Nichols, Hamilton, Parente, Pisco, David Dowell, Andrew Dowell, Mike Ryan, D.J. Funderburk, Will Meyer, Sean Flannery, Jack Flannery, Justin Follmer, Brandon Lerch, Darien Knowles and Frankie Geib.

Special thanks go to Dr. Dan Flannery for reading through the various revisions of the manuscript and offering insight and guidance. Also thanks to Coach Nugent, Jim Kubacki and Tom Glasenapp for giving it patient reads and edits before publication. Also thanks for the photo shoots by K.C. McKenna.

An extended thank you goes to Dan Coughlin for his consultation during the formulation of the book.

For the mind candies, thanks go to Alice Morse Earle, Jim Rohn, Alan Stein, Vince Lomardi, Coach Don Showalter, Ralph Waldo Emerson, Coach Bobby Knight, Henry Kissinger. Brad Stevens, Ben Franklin, The Book of Deuteronomy and others who coined or revised various versions of the inspirational aphorisms.

Jay Bilas and Coach Mike Krzyzewski also get thanks for writing books that provided great inspiration in developing Coach Flannery's coaching philosophy.

A special thanks goes to Joe Scarpitti for all the help he has been in the publication process.

Finally, thanks go to Kaboodle the cat for providing company, as she was resting alongside the computer on the many days while Norm worked through the writings and revisions.

Forward

I have had the good fortune of working with Eric Flannery for many years with USA Basketball teams. Not only is he an outstanding coach but a tremendous person who cares deeply about the players. This book is a journey about Eric and his school during the state championship season. The book will interest not only readers from the St. Edward family but also any coach that has passion for basketball and anyone who wants to learn about leadership development. Readers will find themselves completely immersed in the season as it unfolds to the last-second shot.

When I work with someone closely especially in coaching I get to know him really well. Spending time with Eric was special but also humorous. Many years ago while in Colorado Springs at a training camp I decided to drive to the top of Pikes Peak, which is over 14,000 feet. Eric and several other coaches decided to ride with me. The road was very curvy with no railings to keep the car from tumbling over the side. The ride was great but Eric was not amused by my driving abilities and was extremely happy when we drove down that mountain.

Heights are also a concern for Eric as he does not like looking over the edge of railings or going up in glass elevators. While in Dubai for the USA U-17 World Championships, we thought it would be great to take an elevator up in the tallest building in the world. At the top of the building was an outside glass covered patio that allowed us to see for miles. Eric was actually very good as long as he did not go to the outside edge of the glass lounge. We still give him a hard time about this.

While in Dubai we took a desert safari. We rode in a Land Rover over the sand dunes. Since the sand dunes are very hilly, we went over the dunes like we were on a roller coaster. Our driver turned the radio to a high volume and went over and on the side of many sand dunes.

Much to the dismay of Eric, this went on for at least 30 minutes. The longer the safari continued the more silent Eric became, so when he wanted his barf bag, it was no surprise to the rest of us. He will probably never live that down.

A scary time on one of our trips involved Eric and his passport. Our group all got off the plane and headed to the line for customs to enter the foreign country. As we got to the line, Eric discovered he did not have his passport. He went running back to the plane where he had to get by several security people to get back on the plane. One of the attendants saw Eric in a panic and they both looked for his passport but did not find it on the plane. As Eric went off the plane to head back to the customs line, the attendant was running up to him holding his passport. He had found it on the floor of the plane. This was a sigh of relief for everyone. After that we all asked him if he had his passport.

Despite his acrophobia and aversion to rough rides, Coach Flannery has taken his teams beyond a rocky road and to new heights.

Thanks Coach Flannery for sharing your journey with the rest of us.

– Don Showalter – Head Boys Basketball Coach

Iowa City, City High School

USA Basketball Junior National Teams

Introduction

At the beginning of the 2012-13 season, I had a short conversation with Norm Weber (the beat writer for our basketball team and the school's sports information director) and I had told him that I had always wanted to write a book. I am an avid reader, and I felt it would be great to put some thoughts and ideas into a book. Much to my surprise, Norm said, "I would love to write a book with you." We never spoke of it again until the 2013-14 season had come to an end. It had been a remarkable journey, ending with a "fairy tale" shot at the buzzer to win a state championship. Few would have expected this to play out in real life.

By no means do I believe that I understand anything more than the next guy or that I am a better coach than anyone out there. I simply wanted to try and put a season into text, talk about the journey that the team went on, and share some of my stories and philosophies about the game of basketball.

The reality of this daunting task set in once the championship season was over, and Norm approached me again about writing this book (which I had forgotten all about). The timing could not get much better after winning a state championship, but "time" would be important. I had some idea but never realized the amount of time, skill, and patience one needs to write a book. For all of that I need to send a huge THANK YOU to Norm for spending a tremendous amount of time on this project, listening to my stories, transcribing thousands of words and keeping me on task the best he could.

This entire year could not have been much better for any coach, at any level, as far as winning championships. In a span of thirteen months I won a gold medal in the U-16 FIBA Americas which was held in Uruguay, I won my second state championship in Ohio, and finished off the summer with a World Championship gold medal for the U-17 USA Basketball team, which was held in Dubai. Not a bad year.

I had no idea that the year was going to turn out the way it did, but it was a journey that I will never forget and I am not sure that I will ever have the opportunity to repeat. With that said, I never intended to write a book about how to win championships. I wanted to write about an ordinary basketball season and follow-up with different thoughts on how I approach things in practice, in games, and off the court. It just so happened that this past year turned into something special.

I have always preached about family and enjoying the journey. It could not be more important now than to thank those that have helped me along my journey to this point. There are too many to thank in all; some may be mentioned along the way in this book, but many will go nameless because of time or space. (I certainly have realized in writing a book that one never can get everything he wants on paper. If I were to put it all down, I would have a book of thousands and thousands of pages. That's why we have editors.)

My wife Lori, my high school sweetheart, has been the best coach's wife anyone could ask for. She would do anything for anyone at the drop of a hat. Her heart is bigger than anyone I have ever met. It is nice to have my wife be my best friend, and I have been blessed with that relationship.

My four children, Sean, P.J., Grace and Abigail, as any parent knows, are the center of our universe and are all special to us in their own way. As I have shared with my players over the years, "I treat you like my own children. I love you all the same; I simply like some of you more than others, depending on the day or what you have done."

My mom and dad, who raised eight children of their own, were the best examples of how to be good parents, spouses and role models. My father passed away nine years ago, but is still missed every day, and I certainly wish he could be around to witness not only the games but the growth of his grandchildren.

Thank you to my father and mother in-law, Richard and Kathy Scucs, for always being there for Lori, your grandchildren, and me. Your support has been bountiful.

To my former and current players, you are my extended family. Whether you played 32 minutes a game or never left the bench, you have all been a big part of the St. Edward basketball tradition. You have all been wonderful role-models and as you know, my door is always open. Without you this story cannot be written.

Thanks go to my St. Ed's family, the administration that has always been very supportive of me and the basketball program. It takes a village to raise a child, and they certainly have been supportive in this effort. The faculty and staff at St. Ed's are unbelievable teachers and people who certainly live out the mission of "The Courage to Act." The time and talent they pass along to our students every day is inspiring.

My coaching staff: Jim Flannery, Dan Gallagher, Tom Bodle, Steve Logan, Delvon Blanton, Josh Nugent, Pete Campbell, Joe Scarpitti, Tim Smith, T.J. Gallagher, Fran Gallagher, Jason Bratten, James Crawford, and many others have assisted me over the years. What can I say other than that this is the best coaching staff in the land! I only hire people I trust and these men have been nothing but loyal, hard-working; they each sacrifice a lot of time to help not only myself but our entire program.

I have to also acknowledge the USA Basketball coaches and staff, who I have learned so much from and with whom I have developed life-long relationships: Don Showalter, L.J. Goolsby, B.J. Johnson, Sean Ford, Jim Tooley, Caroline Williams, Samson Kayode, David Craig, and Herb "Doc" Parris. The reason their organization is so successful is because of the people they have involved. Thanks to all for some very memorable experiences.

– St. Edward Head Coach Eric Flannery

Chapter 1

Earned, Not Given

In order for someone to be involved in St. Edward basketball and subsequently get playing time and larger roles on the team, he must buy into the Coach Flannery philosophy, which essentially comes down to his *earning* whatever he gets in the program.

Three areas that are vital for anyone coming into the program are academics, discipline, and personality.

"Someone has to be a quality person and of high character," Coach Flannery said. "Being at a Holy Cross school trying to teach the philosophy of the Holy Cross Brothers, I'm a big believer in giving someone an opportunity even if he struggled academically in grade school. We could be the ones to turn it around for such students."

While the cost of tuition could keep some from even considering St. Ed's, more are unable to get in because of discipline or academic issues.

The school and basketball program have had student-athletes come in to the school only to transfer out after a year or two because it was too tough academically, athletically or disciplinarily.

"Telling someone he can't come to school is crushing to the parent and the student," Coach Flannery said. "It might be the first time in their lives they were told no. We do want those who are athletically talented, but academics and being a good person far outweigh being a good athlete. We want high-character boys that work hard, and represent themselves, their families and the St. Ed's community well."

Flannery does remember well the parents of potential student-athletes who said other coaches have guaranteed that their sons would be starting varsity as freshmen or playing varsity as freshmen. Flannery was the only the coach who has not done that, he would be told.

"That's not our policy," Coach Flannery explained. "Once he gets here, he could play at any level based on his talent and what he earns. We do have talented students here in the school. If I have promised your son, what is to say I have not promised four or five others the same opportunity? We expect all of our student-athletes to earn what they get whether in the classroom for grades or on the playing floor. Some parents didn't like the answer and they wound up going to other schools that guaranteed them spots on the varsity."

On the other side of that were Jawad Williams and Delvon Roe, who did *earn* their spots as freshman varsity players. Coach Flannery had that same conversation with the parents. They were told, "Your son is going to earn everything he gets here. He is going to earn it in the classroom before he gets it on the floor and every minute is going to be *earned* by how he plays." Nothing was given to them through those conversations.

After meeting with Coach Flan, Williams' grandmother called that same night of the meeting and Roe's mother called the same night of her meeting and at two different times essentially both said, "Coach Flan, we have decided already my son is going to St. Edward and I want to let you know why. You are the only coach who did not promise us anything and that our son would *earn* everything he gets and that he would be pushed to be a better student and a better athlete and that's what we want for our son."

They didn't want him to have any hand outs but wanted him to become a better person and a better player.

"When we get a family to commit to that coming in, we know we have them for the right reasons," Coach Flannery said. "Both worked out quite well. Both were being pushed to the limit and both wound up getting high major scholarships while earning everything they were to get."

Williams played on a national championship team at North Carolina, and Roe was in a national championship game with Michigan State.

Roe's father, Delvon Blanton, was an assistant coach on the St. Ed's basketball team that won the state championship in 2013-14. Ten years after his son came into the school, he still remembers the scenario.

"We were looked at by every school around when my son was coming out of the eighth grade," Coach Blanton said. "He and I went to talk to quite a few coaches and sat down in the office with them. They all said this one thing that I remember before I went to St. Edward. They said, 'If you come here, you will start.'

"When I heard that, it threw me off. When I went down to St. Ed's, I sat down with Coach Flannery in his office for the first time and what made my decision that we were going to St. Ed's was when coach said, 'I am not going to guarantee you anything. You earn what you want here. If you continue to work hard, keep your grades up and get better, maybe you'll play here, but I am not going to guarantee you anything.' When I heard Coach Flan say this, I looked him in the eye and said, 'You don't have to worry about my son looking somewhere else. This is where he is going.'"

It's all about putting a son in with adults who *care* about him.

"I wanted to be close to someone who checks on my son and makes him feel wanted," Coach Blanton said. "My son didn't even want to go to St. Ed's at first. I told him he had to go somewhere where someone is going to be on him and teach him discipline and responsibility. To this day, my son tells me that that was the best decision I made for him his entire life."

As it turned out, Roe did wind up starting varsity as a freshman, but that was under unique circumstances.

"Sometimes it's not communicated, but that philosophy would make some people turn their heads," said Tom Bodle, a St. Edward varsity assistant coach. "He might be a hot shot CYO player, but when he comes in, he tries out for the freshman team and then tries out for the JV team; he has to earn his spot and try to prove it on the court. It keeps them away from that entitlement thinking. We might lose some kids. Some might want to hear coming out of eighth grade that they are going to be a varsity player. One of the most talented kids ever to come through here is Delvon Roe. Delvon started on the freshman team in pre-season camp and then was on the JV team. Because we had an injury, all of a sudden we realized we didn't have a big guy."

Roe became the scoring leader as a freshman on varsity that year. After starting the season on the JV team, he earned his move up and chance to show what he could do on the floor, earning the distinction as the scoring leader.

As well as from parents, this also comes from the student-athletes. Tony Vuyancih's (a member of the 2013-14 team) older brother, Joey, played his high school ball at another school and now plays college ball for John Carroll. His dad, Pat Vuyancih, who played on the Cleveland State team that went to the Sweet 16 in the mid 1980s, was somewhat leery about Joey going right to the varsity as a freshman in high school.

"My brother became a starter as a freshman," Vuyancih said. "My dad actually was upset about that. He didn't believe that a freshman deserved to be a starter no matter how skilled. He hadn't earned it yet.

"I had coaches tell me, 'Come here and you will be starting right away.' What really blew my mind was when I was an eighth grader at Coach Flannery's camp. One of his best players stopped showing up and people were saying he was leaving and others said he was staying. Coach Flannery came out and told us, 'Look, I don't care who you are. I am not going to beg you to stay. The guys who want to be here will be here.' That's how it was for me. He wanted us to work for him and for our positions. The other coaches were telling me, you have it right away. They were just going to give it to me. Coach Flan told me subliminally that I was going to have to work for my spot."

Former assistant coaches/players who have moved on to be head coaches, such as Brian Ansberry at Lake Ridge Academy, still recall the fond days at St. Edward when Coach Flannery would not just hand something to a potential St. Ed's student-athlete.

"Coaches at St. Ed's are challenging student-athletes and not handing them anything," Coach Ansberry said. "Some of these kids are constantly, especially in this generation, getting stuff handed to them left and right. 'If you'll play for my team, we'll give you these shoes. You'll get this because you are a really good player.' Everyone is telling them how good they are. Flan comes in and it's a reality check. It's, 'We're a darn good program. If you want to be one of these guys up here on the wall or have a banner up there, you have to work for it.'"

Once a student-athlete has *earned* his role on the St. Ed's basketball team, it is then his job to buy into the philosophy of the program and take ownership of one's role on the team.

"I think as a coach it starts with having a message and continuing to deliver that message," Coach Flannery said. "At some point it is only effective if players buy into it and take ownership. This team (the recent championship team) took ownership. Tony was the vocal leader, and he was constantly getting on his teammates about doing things the right way."

They would also take ownership during the summer months

"During the off season we really bought into it," said Phil Parente, a championship team member who is now attending the University of Cincinnati. "During the off season we were here a lot at 6 in the morning. Even if the coaches weren't here, we were here by ourselves. It was during the summer when we could have slept in, but, considering what happened at the end of the previous season, we trusted in the hard off-season work."

It is not always easy to get the student-athletes to buy into the system.

"Times are changing," Flannery admitted. "It's harder to have these individuals buy into a team sport with social media, Facebook, Twitter, texting and the number of people in different corners telling them one or more things. AAU Basketball plays a role in that. It's a necessary evil, but it is competitive. They have to play summer ball to be noticed by college recruiters."

Any of a number of players on the recent championship team could have scored a lot of points per game, but that would be going outside the system that differentiates St. Edward from other programs.

"A guy like Kipper (Nichols) could score 25 a game on this team and next year maybe he will," Coach Flannery said. "If that's the case, I am not only going to have to sell him on it, I'm going to have to sell the whole team on it. I don't think we have had too many teams on which we had that one guy that is so much better than everybody else."

A lot of that comes from being smart basketball players. The hardest part is not to get student-athletes to sacrifice points but to understand what good shots are.

"Marsalis (Hamilton) could get a shot off any time he wanted," Coach Flannery explained. "That doesn't mean it was a good shot. My thing is teaching my guys to take the best shot for our team not for the individual. If Kipper is wide open, great. He should take the shot. If he is not, Kipper could also dribble 30 times and create a shot. If it means Kipper shoots 15 times and Tony shoots five, so be it. The next game it could be Tony 25 times and Kipper five times. If we get the kids to buy into one another, they share the ball more. They don't get offended when one kid scored 30 and another 10."

If they buy into that team concept, they buy into the "we" idea. Coach Flannery tells his student-athletes that if Kipper hits a jump shot, they all hit a jump shot. That comes natural to them.

"When they share the ball more, they are OK and are accepting more when other people are scoring," Coach Flannery said.

Malcolm Walters, a point guard on the 2013-14 team, was a shooter when he came into the program, but through the help of Steve Logan was turned into a fine point guard before the start of the season.

"Point guard is now my home," Walters explained. "I want to be a point guard but a point guard who can score. I like distributing the ball and getting assists. At first I was all about scoring, but now I like the way assists look. I'm still developing as a point guard. I don't want to stop learning because I want to be the best point guard I can be."

That put a smile on Coach Flannery's face.

"The fact that Malcolm said that (about assists) makes me proud," Coach Flannery said. "Some don't understand it. The reality is that everybody sees the point (scoring) guy. It's our job as coaches to make everyone on the team understand the importance of every thing and buy into it. Maybe there are one or two rebounders who are the best rebounders they could possibly be, getting 8, 10, 12 rebounds a game. That's their goal and we have to make it something that is exciting to them. We have to make them understand that it is just as important as scoring 20 points. It is convincing a guy like Malcolm that getting an assist is just as important as getting the basket, because he has made that happen.

"That also builds the thought, 'I don't have to score 20 points today; I'm going to try to get 10 rebounds. I feel good about myself and I feel good about my team winning.' Marsalis Hamilton really bought into that this year. He sacrificed this year. That made us better and made us closer as a team. The year before as a junior, he didn't understand that. We lost in the district championship versus winning the state championship. There is a difference in buying into it."

Walters also bought into the "*earning* what one gets" concept.

"I wouldn't want to come to a school where they just give it to me; I like to be challenged," Walters said. "I feel more accomplished if I really have to work for it. Coming here was so great because it wasn't handed to me. I had to work for a spot. Coach Flan told me I would not get this spot off the bat. I might still get it, but I'd have to work for it. It was challenging to be given the spot because I worked hard for it. It was more satisfying. He didn't just say, here Malcolm here's a spot for just coming here. Life is not like that. This prepares us for life. In life we have to work for everything, and we have to pay a price for everything."

The championship team of 2014 was made possible in a large part to the contribution of Kipper Nichols, who eventually matured into a high-major prospect.

"Coach Flan got a lot of flak for not starting Kipper in the ninth grade," Coach Blanton said. "Some schools were saying that, 'If you were here Kipper, you would be starting. He's not going to let you start.' I told Kipper and his mom after this year, 'Didn't I tell you that if Kipper came here, he was going to be special and he was going to win?' His mom said, 'Delvon you did say that.' I said, 'I told you; you always have to put your son in a position in which someone cares for him and someone is going to do right for him.' When Kipper first started here, Kipper was spoiled and Kipper didn't know how to work hard. Look at Kipper now. It took time for him to grow. It took a special coach to bring that out. He could have gone to a lot of other good programs. He could have gone somewhere he would have played a lot right off the bat. If he would have gone to some of those other places, Kipper would have done what he wanted to do. That's not the case here. When someone comes here, he is accountable for everything he does. He has to compete for every minute he gets on that floor. If he's not going to do it, Flan has the guts to pull his best player off the floor and sit him down. That's something that a lot of coaches won't do."

Earning their keeps, buying into the system and taking ownership has helped St. Ed's student-athletes succeed after their high school careers.

"When I say that to not only the kid but to the parent and they still come here, I know I have them and I know I have them for the right reasons," Coach Flannery explained. "The parents who come here know that that's the score. Every parent deep down wants what's best for his or her teen and for that student to be successful and he or she wants his or her child to play. Parents say, 'You told us our son will earn it. I appreciate that and that's why he is here.' He wasn't expecting anything. He knows that if he does play or does not play, it is because of his own merit. If he doesn't, it wasn't because we promised him anything and he didn't get that. Those are the people who are true to themselves and truly want what is best. They buy into that and trust it.

"We've had a lot of compliments, especially from parents of guys who have had success in life. They have said things that my son is where he is today because he earned what he got. Some didn't buy into it and went elsewhere. I have alternative candidates. He may not be as talented as one player, but if he works as hard, he's just as good because he's doing it all for all the right reasons. He's going to run through that wall for me rather than complaining or moaning about his playing time."

Someone such as Tony Vuyancih claiming he came to St. Ed's because he wanted to earn his spot gives credence to the idea that people are buying into the notion of no hand outs.

"We have someone who knows what he is going to get," Coach Flannery said. "We know what we are getting from him. If the person next to him is promised something, one would see it in his effort. One would see it in his attitude and spoiled nature. When I hear a student-athlete say, 'I am here because I am going to earn it and earn everything I have,' then I know I am getting a student-athlete who is buying into me and buying into the team and buying into his hard work. When I hear it from the student-athlete, I know I have him and he's a great teammate."

Earning the success all becomes a part of being "worthy of the jersey" and playing for something greater than themselves.

Chapter 2

Playing For Something Greater Than Themselves

In order to get student-athletes to buy into the team concept, coaches must inject into them a selfless seed that allows them to see that playing for something greater than themselves will bring outstanding rewards. Individually, players have to be worthy of what they get by earning it. They must realize that they have spiritual, mental and physical gifts that are unique. Others, who might not have the same assets, might just have the gift of inspiration.

During the first day of practice for the 2013-14 season, the St. Edward basketball team got together and the coaches had them write down what "worthy of the jersey" meant to them. The theme of the 2013-14 team was "Worthy of the Jersey." It was part of the school's slogan for the year, "Worthy of the Call."

Each student-athlete on the basketball team was prepared to write a one-to-two-page essay on this worthy-of-the-jersey concept. This one, like the mind candy, was to test their mental skills. This group of student-athletes, with a team grade point average of 3.6, was worthy of the assignment.

"It should be an honor and a privilege to represent the St. Edward community," senior Connor Pisco said. "St. Ed's is a program a lot of schools would like to be like. The former coaches and players have set this reputation that we need to continue. We have to do the same every time we put on the same jersey they wore."

Senior point guard Malcolm Walters had a clever way of putting it.

"You are not playing for the name on the roster but for the name on the front of the jersey," Walters said. "Having a skill set can take you only so far, but being a teammate can take you as far as you allow it because teammates fight for one another and believe in one another."

To Walters, putting on the jersey meant being part of a brotherhood, a family and a bond.

"Putting on a St. Edward jersey means you are no longer playing for yourself, but for the name on the jersey and for the family," Walters wrote. "Putting on the jersey means looking at the big picture and that is that we are one."

Junior pivot man Mike Ryan found three key principles in putting on the jersey: 1) forming a good relationship with peers, 2) avoiding conflict and 3) enjoying yourself and having fun when playing.

"As a devoted player you must be committed; it's important to show up to practice in your appropriate practice gear and be on time," Ryan wrote. "During game time, whether you are in the game or not, you should be encouraging and supportive of your teammates. Lastly you should be committed to bettering yourself as a basketball player. Set goals for yourself and your team, and work hard to accomplish those goals. As a team player, I need to know my role on the team. Never come out of that role, and accept the role given by the coach."

For Marsalis "Sal" Hamilton, it was a matter of getting rid of selfishness.

"Being worthy of the jersey means respecting not only the program but the school," Hamilton wrote. "We must completely get rid of any selfishness or lack of effort. Worthy of the jersey means to sacrifice my own pride and mindset and to prove to others and ourselves that we as a team are worthy enough to put on the same jerseys of those who paved the way for us."

Since being worthy of the jersey is about being team oriented, all members of that team count and such a slogan helps bond the team.

"Guy No.1 puts on the same jersey as guy No. 15," guard Phil Parente said. "The 15 guy means just as much to the team as the No. 1 guy does.

The jersey stands for a team, group, union and we need to treat it like that and be a team. We have to ask, 'Do we pick each other up and motivate one another? Do we work as hard for not only ourselves but for our school, coaches, classmates, players from the past and alumni? Do we work together as a team?' If we answer yes to these questions, then we are Worthy of the Jersey."

Will Meyer had a definition for someone who might *not* be worthy of the jersey.

"If one is not worthy of the jersey, then he simply does not have the desire to succeed," said Meyer, also the No. 1 singles player on the 2014 tennis team. "We cannot have the desire just sometimes; we have to have it all the time. Then it is likely that good things will happen."

For some, there is an immediate family heritage to wearing the St. Ed's jersey.

"I have gone to St. Ed's games since I can remember," wrote Jack Flannery. "I always wanted to play basketball at St. Edward. When I got to school here, I realized it was not going to be easy and it would take a lot of hard work. In 2012-13 we took putting on the St. Ed's jersey for granted. It made me contemplate what I needed to do for this season. Kids at other schools would love to be in our position and playing for St. Ed's. It comes back to being worthy of the jersey. We are here for a reason and that is to win the state championship."

For Flannery, being worthy of the jersey meant loyalty, commitment, dedication, composure and humility.

"We should treat the jersey and everything that comes with it as our most prized possession," wrote Justin Follmer. "By putting on the jersey, we are part of St. Ed's history."

Pat Riley, the second point guard, looked at it in a way that asks the question, "When we come back in 10 or 15 years, how would we like to see our former program?" Riley emphasized the word "together" when discussing the worthy of the jersey aspect of it.

"When making my decision to pick a high school, I know I could have picked a lot of programs where I would be the leading scorer," Tony Vuyancih wrote. "I wanted to earn what I received and could do that only at St. Edward. Two of my greatest idols, Delvon Roe and Myles Hamilton, taught me what worthy of the jersey means. Delvon seemed so kind and down to earth. Myles represented the heart and will to win. Between the two, I learned that 'Worthy of the Jersey' means that it is earned and once you have it, be humble and give everything you can.

"Those were the guys I saw growing up playing for St. Ed's. I always had this idea that St. Ed's is a great basketball program. Those are the ones that really put the name to the jersey. It was our job to uphold the same standards by playing hard and playing together and doing them proud, as we would want when we come back in the next 10 to 20 years. We'd all want to see the St. Ed's we played for instead of as if it were a different program. We wouldn't want the kids just playing for themselves or something else."

To Andrew Dowell, it meant to be not only better players but "better men" in being worthy of the jersey.

"There is nothing more that I want to do than to help bring my school a state championship," Dowell said. "I go to work every day to accomplish this."

His twin brother, David Dowell, believes to be worthy one must represent the school in a positive manner.

"It is important to give 110 percent in everything we do on the court," David Dowell wrote. "Many players in the history of St. Ed's have given their all, and it is important that we carry on the legacy."

Being worthy of the jersey is evident at games, but it could also be something that student-athletes would want to take pride in while out in public.

"While out to eat the other day, I had a random guy come up to me while I was wearing my St. Ed's jacket and he asked me about past teams and our current team," junior Frankie Geib wrote. "Our program has become well known and respected and it is our turn to carry on the tradition and put on our stamp on this legacy that is St. Edward basketball."

For junior Darien Knowles, it is a matter of what kind of person emerges from one who is worthy of the jersey.

"By going to St. Ed's, it shows for the most part a guy holds a certain amount of morals and intentions within himself," Knowles wrote. "A lot of outside people look up to us. There is way more than talent that plays into being a good player/person/role model."

Brandon Lerch found worthy of the jersey to mean an "acceptance of my second family, a brotherhood." Kipper Nichols said being worthy of the jersey is being thankful to be in a position that others are not and to surpass one's own high expectations.

D.J. Funderburk looked at putting on a St. Ed's jersey as having a target on his back, which meant having more pressure to play harder and work harder to represent well the alumni who wore the jersey before him, as well as his school and family.

"Nothing is ever guaranteed by putting on that jersey," said Sean Flannery, who along with Funderburk, were the only sophomores on the team. "I am sure that if I asked any past player that came through St. Ed's if he would like to put on the jersey one last time, he would say yes in a heart beat. Putting on the jersey that says 'St. Edward' across the front is something special."

While all of them had something to say about the "worthy-of the-jersey" slogan, they realized they had to use their gifts for someone who because of limitations could not do what they could do. They decided that they were going to prove themselves worthy by winning the state championship for "Big Mike" Orbany, the younger brother of St. Edward team manager Matt Orbany. Big Mike, who was one of the biggest fans of St. Edward student-athletics, was stricken with brain and spinal cancer.

On May 1, 2014, Big Mike Orbany lost his battle with cancer and passed away, but he was a winner all the way and a big inspiration to the Eagles' winning ways in all sports. Mike Orbany was the MVP and captain. He was nine.

The players at the final four wore T-shirts that said, "Eagles Soar for Big Mike" and NEGU (Never Ever Give Up). Big Mike was not at the game, but he was able to watch it on TV. It was one of the last things he witnessed in his life. The wake was held at the St. Edward Chapel, and the line wound around the street all the way up to Bunts Road (three blocks down).

"The guys bought into one another, liked one another and wanted to play for one another," Coach Flannery said. "To have things that kept us grounded and focused might have meant more to some people than it did to others, but a guy like Michael allowed us to take a step back and appreciate what we have. We understand that it puts things into perspective – it's just a game. Guys are fighting for their lives. We're not fighting for our lives. It allows these guys to fight for something that is bigger than just a game."

Michael was a student at St. Bernadette in Westlake. Several of the players and Coach Flannery, who lost his father Jim to cancer, showed up at the school and did Clips for Cancer, having their heads shaved. Michael Orbany was present.

A Guinness World Record was attempted for number of haircuts done by a team of 10 in one hour. The event raised funds and awareness for cancer research through The St. Baldrick's Foundation. The school broke the record for most haircuts.

"It is also part of that Holy Cross mission," Coach Flannery said. "We were helping Michael as much as Michael was helping us. Our guys learned from Michael -- how it is to be tough and the battle he had been going through. We had something else to play for."

Michael's brother, Matt, who is a team manager, was at practice every single day and was committed to the team and doing his job while all this was going on in his personal life. He didn't make it a burden on anyone else.

"We had to ask Matt how things were going to get information out of him," Coach Flannery said.

When the team went to the final four, Matt approached the team and asked the guys if they would do him a favor for his brother and wear the T-shirts in his honor. The players didn't hesitate. They said absolutely.

Coach Flannery was a pall bearer at the funeral for Mike Orbany.

"The ultimate end is going to happen at some point but it still doesn't make it any easier," Coach Flannery said the next day. "There was sadness. Just to see parents losing their child, nine years old, no matter what the situation, is tough. We just try to remember him for what he left. The biggest thing that stands out to me is how, in such a short period of time, a person could make that much of a difference. That's the life lesson we have. It isn't necessarily how long we are here; it's what a person does with that time. It's what is given to other people. His legacy will be remembered for that.

"He was a part of something. It wasn't just basketball, but also football and the St. Ed's community. Even though he wasn't a student here himself, he felt a part of our community. We always talk about family and building relationships."

It was Kipper Nichols who said that he realizes he had been given by God a lot more than many other people, and there was no reason not to use his talent to the fullest to accomplish the goal, not only for his own community and family but for someone who didn't have as many physical and mental gifts, someone such as Mike Orbany.

"One cannot be in a Holy Cross school and at a Catholic school and not think that way," Coach Flannery said. "To be in a situation like this is another example of a way to teach our guys. Basketball is not a matter of life or death. There are more important things and that's another lesson that I took from Big Mike. What's the worst thing that could happen to us? We could lose a basketball game somewhere down the line. This boy was battling for his life every day, and we are so entrenched in what we are doing that we sometimes don't put things into perspective."

While they still had Big Mike for the season and had given deep thought into what being "worthy of the jersey," truly means, they had the inspirational makings to go out and have a successful season.

Chapter 3

Jumping Out to an Eye-Opening Start

The 2013-14 St. Ed's basketball season really started at the end of the 2012-13 campaign, when St. Ed's had a team with potential but one lacking in team chemistry. A lot of learning took place during the offseason to create greater chemistry.

Entering the 2012-13 season, St. Ed's had won seven district championships in the eight previous seasons. The No. 1-seeded Eagles had been upset by North Royalton, 53-51, in the 2012-13 district championship game. The Eagles had been without two of their top outside shooters in juniors Malcolm Walters and Tony Vuyancih, a team captain. This group was now hungry.

"There didn't seem to be a lot of camaraderie (with the 2012-13 team)," Coach Flannery said. "They just didn't play well together."

The loss to North Royalton was used as a motivating tool for the championship season. Although it is a good strategy to use a long-lasting loss as a motivator, it still needs to be guarded. "We could over do it even though we try not to," Coach Flannery said. It kept the team's eye on the prize, living up to being worthy of the jersey. In a paradoxical way, the loss was a gift.

"I think there is way more positive that came out of that loss than negative," Coach Flannery said. "It might be one of the better things that happened to us."

Such as it is, it came down to doing all the right things within the system and turning a negative outcome into positive energy.

"It starts at the end of the previous season," Coach Flannery said.

So during the off season, they set a goal to win a state championship and made it a project to improve in all areas they needed to in order to do so. The team would learn from 2012-13 and have big night after big night throughout the season.

"We had a big win against Mater Dei (in January 2013). After that we went downhill," Coach Flannery said. "They patted themselves on the back and said, 'We are good, and we beat one of the best teams in the country.' Things started unraveling and sure enough, we lose in the district championship."

All great seasons at St. Edward have had great moments and big victories but only two have led to state championships. It's usually not individual games for which teams are remembered.

"In 2007 they remember that we made it to the final four," Coach Flannery recalled. "In 2008 they remember we made it to the state championship game. We didn't care that we lost six games during the year. Nobody remembers it. This team is going to be remembered for winning the state championship."

Brian Ansberry, a member of the '98 state championship team, was an assistant coach at St. Ed's through the spring of 2013 before taking the head position at Lake Ridge Academy.

"Two and a half weeks into open gyms, they were into it," Ansberry said. "In years past they would lose and just think of it as another thing. These guys wanted to get right back at it. We almost said the 2012-13 team could beat anyone, but they could also lose to anyone, depending on attitude. Some days they are just world beaters like against Mater Dei, but then in other games they struggled. When we lost in the district, it stung and hurt because we had not lost a district in so long."

So the North Royalton loss was behind them. It was now the next play, the next game, the next season.

During the 2012-13 season, St. Ed's had a steady point guard in Royal Eddie, who went on to play Division III ball at Mount Union. He was backed up by then junior Pat Riley, also a defensive back on the football team that was ranked No. 1 in Ohio for parts of both the 2012 and 2013 seasons. Pat had started a handful of games in place of Eddie.

Riley could have been the starter on the 2013-14 team, but the Eagles were in a position of having three shooting guards that would be good candidates as starters and only two point guards in Riley and Sean Flannery, the coach's son, who as a freshman was the JV point guard in 2012-13, but as a sophomore was still too young to take on the reigns as the starter.

Riley would not join the team until after the football season, which could have gone as far as December. As it was it went on until late November. It was determined early that Walters, a wing on the 2012-13 team, would become a point guard. The move for Walters, a senior, was not easy, but he was willing to accept and embrace his new role at point guard.

Working with him was Steve Logan, who had returned to help the team just at the right time. Logan, who directed a state championship team in 1998 from the point-guard position, had been in and out since graduating from St. Ed's in 1998, but finally came back to offer input at the start of the 2013-14 season.

"The point guard is the coach on the floor," Coach Flannery said. "He's the guy I look to for answers. He's the guy I blame for just about anything that goes on in a game."

Without a point guard, the gas that runs the engine is missing and the whole ride winds up being a bumpy one if not a broken down one.

"As the leader of the team, the point guard runs the show," Coach Flannery said. "If I were asked if there came a point when I was comfortable with Malcolm as the point guard, the honest answer is that I don't think I was ever 100 percent sold even up to the state championship game, but I don't think I am sold on any player."

Walters, on the other hand, was 100 percent sold on himself and went into the season with confidence.

"The shooting guard is my more natural position," Walters said. "I knew I would have to be a point guard at some point and that's what coach asked me to do. I took on the role to help the team. It's a tough position to learn. I still haven't reached my maximum potential at it. Mr. Logan coming back really helped me a lot, considering he had made it as far as he did in Division I and the NBA," Walters said. "His knowledge of the position really helped me to become a point guard."

Part of this project was turning Walters into a leader out top.

"With the way I saw Malcolm work, I knew this could be a really good thing for us," Coach Flannery said. "Malcolm had always had talent to play. He could score. He had great athleticism. He could do a lot of things other people can't do even though he wasn't a true point guard. My biggest concern was whether he could be the leader we needed."

The first thing he needed to do was lead by example. In the off season, Flannery saw that developing in him. Although Walters worked as hard as anybody, during the summer before the championship season, he still needed to start talking. He needed to start telling people where to go. He did. He was buying into becoming more vocal. He was becoming a leader. Some might say that leadership cannot be taught. If that were the case, then all the colleges and universities in the country might as well shut down all their MBA programs.

"That is one of the things I continue to learn as a coach," Coach Flannery said. "People say leaders are born and not made. Certain qualities like a sense to see the big picture or a knack to should collective responsibility are innate, but we can help build leaders. We can teach them certain ways to talk to people. Malcolm is the perfect example."

While leadership molding had several steps, there were two main parts.

"A guy like Steve Logan got it into his mind in a different way," Coach Flannery said. "Then it is the head coach teaching him different things and different responsibilities. He became a leader."

When things did not always go well with Walters, there was always Riley who could step in to take a leadership role, which often did happen.

"We had some moments and times when he (Walters) might have taken a step back because he lost some confidence in himself. How he responded to those moments I thought was really good," Coach Flannery said. "He really showed he could be a point guard from the beginning. As a coach, I liked the security blanket of having a Pat Riley, who could settle things down since he had played the back-up position the previous year."

Actually Riley had more experience in that point-guard position than Walters even though he was coming off the bench. In a sense, it was a point-guard-by-committee situation. In many games during the season, the starting five would build a big lead and the second five with Riley at the point would keep things going, even building on the leads at times.

"All along we knew we could be good at that position between the two of them," Coach Flannery said. "When we put those two together, we had our ideal point guard. We had a guy a little more point-guard minded in Pat Riley and more fundamentally sound in the way he handled the ball and played defense. Then we had Malcolm, an athlete and a scorer, who had the basketball skill to do different things."

The Riley-Walters melding was so significant that Riley, a senior, was one of the four team captains. Having a non-starter as a captain said a lot for how deep this team was.

"Since I didn't get back from football season that first Monday before the first game, I talked with Coach Flan coming into the season and he said he wanted me to be a captain," Riley said. "He told me how he wanted me to emerge more like a leader this year. He holds his point guards to a higher standard. We're almost like his coach on the floor. He expects us to get into the offense and hold them accountable to make sure everyone is going to the right place."

Once they had the point guard situation straightened out, the St. Edward coaching staff was ready to start practicing for the 2014 season. They knew they would have to be ready because this would be one of the most challenging seasons in school history. Because St. Ed's has not been in a league (for most sports) since the early 1970s, its sports teams play an independent schedule and thus are not really playing for anything during the regular season. They play for only one thing – to win the state championship. Coach Flannery in pre-season interviews let it be known that winning during the regular season is nice, but the clear purpose of playing a regular season at St. Edward is to prepare for the post season.

"I've said this and I mean it; this is the strongest schedule we have ever put together," Coach Flannery said before the season started. "We could go 11-11 and play extremely well, but we will be ready to make a run in the tournament."

As Riley and reserves Andrew Dowell, David Dowell, and Frankie Geib could attest, St. Edward's football team has to play a strong schedule in order to make the playoffs.

"It's not like football in which we have to establish computer points," Coach Flannery said. "I don't care if we go 22-0 or 18-4; I just want to be as good as we can be come March. Our schedule is going to prepare us for that."

The schedule included two preparatory schools that educate post-graduates who are student-athletes, Huntington St. Joseph Prep out of West Virginia and Hargrave Academy out of Virginia. This would bring 13th graders, those 19 years old, to play against St. Ed's. This didn't concern Coach Flannery. The idea was to learn, improve and situationally react well. Hargrave had eight Division I players who were older and most of them taller than the St. Ed's group, but that did not concern the coaches, players, student body, or fans. They wanted a winner and if it meant playing tough competition and losing, then so be it. The goal was to win the state championship and not to beat up on opponents that didn't stand a chance. Huntington St. Joseph Prep (and its forerunner and host school St. Joseph Central Catholic High School) was well known for sending a number of its basketball student-athletes to Division I programs such as Texas Tech, University of Cincinnati, West Virginia, Louisville, Kansas, Memphis, Cleveland State, Ole Miss, Illinois, New Mexico State, and Florida State. The Eagles were also scheduled to play in one of the top tournaments in the country, the MaxPreps Holiday Classic over Christmas break in Palm Springs, California. They knew they were going to get some of the toughest competition in the country. As it turned out, the Eagles played three of the top 20 ranked teams in the country at the tournament.

In addition to Riley and Walters at point guard, the Eagles had Hamilton, Vuyancih, and Nichols returning as potential starters. Also back was part-time starting center Mike Ryan, who had made a rapid progression from being on the freshman team in 2011-12, to being part time JV/part time varsity for the first few games of 2012-13, to being full time varsity for most of the season. The Eagles were expecting big things out of Ryan.

While the Eagles had some solid players who were ready to be starters, the Eagles' bench would make the difference during this championship season. In addition to Riley running things from the point when Walters was out, the Eagles had 6-9 sophomore Derek (D.J.) Funderburk, who had played center on the JV team as a freshman. Funderburk, a Division I prospect, was being brought along slowly. At the start of this season his designated role was to give the team height, rebounding, shot blocking and general defensive intimidation off the bench. Also there was Will Meyer to bring relief at forward. Also back was Phil Parente, a senior outside shooter who could nail a three in clutch situations. Pure athletes in the Dowell twins, who had fine JV years in 2012-13, would add crucial depth for a team that could put any of its players on the floor and maintain or build upon a lead.

"If we were to compare this year's team to last year's team, we do have more depth," Coach Flannery said at the start of the season.

One characteristic of most of Flannery's teams at St. Ed's is that there is rarely one prolific scorer who carries the load. The team's leading scorer usually averages between 12 and 14 points a game. This held true this season more than any other. Instead of the normal 12-15 players, this team included 18 varsity players. When it came down to the final five or six players, the coaches couldn't decide who to cut so they kept more than the usual number. They felt that everyone could add something to the ultimate goal of winning the state championship. They weren't just being "nice guys" and keeping people because they didn't want to hurt their feelings. All 18 would have a role in this championship season.

"Every year our focus is a state championship," Coach Flannery said. "The regular season to me is practice; it's getting exposure to different situations; it's playing and walking away with confidence when playing good teams.

"It's also getting their teammates to like them," Coach Flannery said. "That's everybody. How are these guys going to buy into one another? To me, that's just as important as how they play on the floor and how talented they are. That was my biggest concern: are we going to get along and play well together so that we could compete for a state championship."

St. Edward's basketball team starts its season later than most teams since its football and soccer teams usually go deep into the playoffs. As a rule, the regular season does not start until December, but there are still scrimmages in November.

One scrimmage that stood out as a learning tool for the 2013-14 season was at Holy Name. The Eagles were playing a team that plays against mostly middle-division schools; but, as a Catholic school, Holy Name typically has enough talent to make it a challenging pre-season experience for St. Edward. While the Eagles learned some things in terms of X's and O's, they learned much more about leadership and collective accountability. The lesson helped keep the team together all the way until the end of March, when the final buzzer sounded in Columbus.

Hamilton, who was one of a few to have played varsity as a freshmen at St. Edward, was now a senior. He was expected to be one of the captains along with Riley, Vuyancih and Walters. This meant he had to lead by example. Whatever went for him went for the rest of the team. The team was more important than individual accolades. This meant winning and losing with dignity. It also meant showing respect for the game and for the opponent. Holy Name was to be part of Hamilton's education as a leader.

"It's proportional," Hamilton said. "If coach tells Malcolm one thing, it applies to all of us. It's one thing. Coach Flan does a great job of letting us be vocal overall. He sets the standard that if you don't know what you are doing, you're not playing. We have to know. Communication is one of the biggest things for us."

If a student-athlete sees and hears something being told to a captain, he should know that it goes for everyone. Moreover, the captain has to take that advice the right way, or it will never get channeled to the other ranks of the team.

"If I am talking to a player, I expect everyone else to be listening so that they don't make the same mistake," Coach Flannery explained. "It doesn't always work out that way, but I don't want to repeat myself. Marsalis came to understand this and this is why he became a great leader."

Such a captain also has to know how to take a learning opportunity from a coach and turn it into a leadership opportunity for himself.

"He (Hamilton) knew when things weren't going great; I could pick on him and he knew how to take it, and he knew I wasn't just yelling at him," Flannery said. "I am getting my frustration out on everybody and he took it the right way. Everybody else would take it the right way."

Instead of going to a "born leader" and saying "here, lead," this development of leadership within this team proved to be pivotal throughout the season.

"When a team has a guy like that who is arguably one of our best players who can take it, we have something," Flannery said. "Tony was a guy like that. I knew I could get on those guys and make a point. I might be yelling at our best guys not to play selfishly or to play harder. Everybody else should get the message."

There was a big moment in that scrimmage at Holy Name.

"It's Holy Name and our guys think we are St. Ed's and they are Holy Name and we should win," Flannery recalled. "I don't focus on winning or losing in scrimmages. It's just about getting guys playing time. We were winning, and Marsalis was not playing hard and wanted to focus elsewhere. He wanted to play to the crowd. He thought that this was just a scrimmage. Toward the end of the scrimmage he was out there making himself look foolish."

Flannery took this as a coaching moment and realized if the team would achieve its ultimate goal, he needed to nip this attitude in the bud. He sensed a leader acting uncharacteristically as a non-leader.

"He was playing selfishly and laughing and not playing hard," Flannery said. "This was literally the last two minutes, the clock was running out and he was screwing around. I didn't say a word. I was just staring at him."

Sometimes body language gets a message across much better than words.

"All the kids on the bench were looking at me and wondering what is going on," Flannery continued to explain. "In my head, I said that this was going to be a defining moment on this team right now. Either Marsalis is going to be with us, or he is not. We shook hands with Holy Name, walked off the court and went back into the locker room."

If they were going to live up to their championship aspirations, the edict had to come down at this point.

"I closed the door and locked it. I spent maybe ten minutes ripping into Marsalis in front of the entire team about being selfish and immature.

I reminded him how he was supposed to be the leader of this team. I told him if this is going to be how it is for him or anybody else on this team, don't come back tomorrow," Flannery explained. "It was one of the most frustrating moments we had all year."

It doesn't matter if it is in a practice, in a scrimmage or a game, the leaders and everyone else are going to be serious. Leaders were needed to show everybody how to act the right way. Flannery also went into a couple other guys for not stopping Marsalis.

"It was the others' responsibility to tell Marsalis to be serious and grow up," Coach Flannery said. "After that they came back and focused and worked hard. It was one of those moments when Marsalis said, 'Coach is getting on me, but he is telling everyone else that this is the way it needs to happen.'"

Hamilton said that he was going to be the guy to take the brunt of the criticism, which he admitted he deserved. He was going to be the Mensch. That moment helped carry the team the rest of the season.

With the leadership lesson well in hand, the regular season was set to begin on Dec. 7 at John Adams High School. During the game, D.J. Funderburk came down with a rebound and went hard to the floor with a member of John Adams' team. Right after, the John Adams bench cleared and a number of fans came down from the stands. A brawl on the floor ensued. Finally, things were restored to sanity and the game continued. Part of the problem was lack of security for the game. When the police finally did arrive, they admitted that they were not even aware that a game was taking place that afternoon. A few players were suspended for competition and more than a dozen John Adams students were suspended from school.

The brawl angered the St. Edward basketball team. The Eagles rolled to a 94-39 win against the Rebels and set the tone in two ways: 1) it was to be an example of the dominance the team was capable of through the rest of the season and 2) it brought back a memory for those who had been around St. Ed's basketball for many years. The latter served as a silver lining in the cloud in an otherwise tough situation. During the first state championship season of 1997-98, the Eagles opened the season against Mount Zion. In that game, a brawl erupted and the Eagles went on to win, 63-56. So both championship seasons not only had Steve Logan involved (first as a player and then as a team helper), but both also started with a brawl.

The team concept rang true in this game as four student-athletes reached double figures for the Eagles. Vuyancih had a game-high 22 points, including four three pointers, while Walters added 16, Hamilton 15 and Nichols 11. The 55-point win was significant in that it did not come against a weak opponent. Adams had come into the game with a 2-0 record fresh off a big win against Bedford, which was considered one of the best teams in the Cleveland area.

"I was proud that our kids stayed on the bench and did not get involved in the incident," Coach Flannery said after the game.

Beginning the season with a blowout victory left some people believing that the 2013-14 St. Ed's basketball team could be a powerful one. The big test was still to come with the Palm Springs trip; but in the interim the Eagles had two games left to play before embarking for the West. Pre-Christmas games were slated against St. Vincent-St. Mary and Warrensville Heights, both ranked in the Cleveland area. St. Vincent-St. Mary is the Akron school that claims NBA star LeBron James as a distinguished alumnus.

The Eagles dominated St. V., jumping out to a 10-0 lead to start the game and never trailing. However, the Irish did not lie down easily, making it a close game several times. The Eagles hit a cold spell in the second quarter and St. V. was able to cut its deficit to one point on three occasions.

The bench was to play a factor in this one, setting the tone for a season in which depth would be one of the central attributes of this team. Will Meyer came off the bench to play hounding defense and score a few baskets in the second quarter, enabling the Eagles to boost the lead back to 10 points by halftime.

They took the Irish out of their game and were able to convert on transition baskets, eventually rolling to a 72-59 win. Again the depth manifested itself in the scoring. Unselfish play produced four double-figure scorers for the second game in a row. Nichols scored 19, Hamilton 13, Vuyancih 12 and Meyer 11. "It's going to be someone different every night," Coach Flannery said. "Kipper Nichols or Malcolm Walters or Tony or Hamilton can score 25 on any given night." It again reemphasizes that aspect of the St. Edward tradition of balanced scoring, unselfish play, and sacrificing for the team.

The Eagles were supposed to play at the University of Detroit Jesuit High School this same weekend, but the game was called off when weather conditions made it unsafe for the Eagles to travel north. Eight days later was Warrensville Heights. Again the Eagles jumped out to a quick lead and made the opponent play catch-up the entire night.

This time the early lead was 8-0, but unlike St. V., the Tigers were never really able to make a game of it. This left some wondering how good this Eagle team could be. The Eagles led by 10 points most of the first half and by 20 most of the second half on the way to an 81-52 win.

The distribution in the scoring was again evident as three reached double figures in scoring: Hamilton with 23, Vuyancih with 17 and Nichols with a baker's dozen. Hamilton as the leading scorer again illustrated again what Coach Flannery said previously about having a different leading scorer on any given night.

"Even without pressing, we are still scoring 78 points a game," Coach Flannery said after the game.

While the Eagles were starting to like the idea of jumping out early, it probably wasn't going to happen every week, and there was always the chance of squandering a huge lead.

"I hope we could jump out to a lead like that 30 times," Coach Flannery said. "It would be nice to get used to that, but it could lead to some complacency once the game gets late."

It was certain that close games were going to abound. Still, the Eagles had confidence that they could be the better team in any given game.

With a 3-0 record, the Eagles were set for their flight to California to play four teams, at least three of whom were ranked nationally. The MaxPreps Holiday Classic is one of the most prestigious in the nation. Going on a long trip of more than 2,000 miles from home is not something every basketball team gets to do. It is not something St. Ed's does every year, but for the 2013-14 season, Flannery and his coaching staff wanted to take on the hefty challenge against four national-level teams.

"Every time I've had a team go away on a trip like that we come back better and closer," Coach Flannery said. "We know more about one another off the floor, even if it is just one student-athlete on the team building a relationship with another student-athlete. That makes the team stronger because they have bonded. We did some things together to build that camaraderie and relationships," Coach Flannery said. "When we beat a team in these tournaments, it built our confidence."

The Eagles did indeed return home from the Christmas trip with more confidence after winning three of four games and taking fifth place in the 24-team tournament. Most of the teams they played had already played double or triple the number of games the Eagles had played.

"When we look back, we could have won that tournament," Coach Flannery said. "We ended up playing the better teams in the tournament."

The Eagles had a first-round bye before playing SunnySlope from Phoenix, Arizona in the second round. SunnySlope came into the game 9-0, having defeated Junipero Serra of California in the first round.

St. Ed's handed SunnySlope its first loss of the season, 72-70, with a nice run at the end of the first quarter to take a 19-13 lead and then building a 14-point lead by halftime, 44-30. Three Eagles reached double figures with Hamilton scoring 20, Nichols 10, and Ryan 10.

The Eagles would be challenged by playing two games in one day. The SunnySlope game was played early in the morning; the game against Westchester from Los Angeles would be played at night.

Westchester is an area of LA that is best known as the home of the 1960s musical group The Turtles, otherwise known as Flo & Eddie. Westchester also boasts a pretty good high school basketball program, having won the MaxPreps Holiday Classic in 2012.

For the first time of this season the Eagles would go down in defeat, 66-58, to Westchester, falling to 4-1 on the season. The Eagles dug a hole for themselves, shooting under 20 percent both from the field and at the line in the first half. After trailing by as many as 21 points, the Eagles did narrow the deficit. Nichols had 14 points and Hamilton 12.

Surviving the two-games-in-a-day situation, the Eagles would bounce back in the back draw of the tournament. More importantly, Coach Flannery would make a statement before the next game that anything done on the court would be done for the team.

To prove that the team comes first, Coach Flannery benched two of his top players in Marsalis Hamilton and Kipper Nichols in the second half.

Both played the first half. Nichols was in foul trouble and Hamilton had six points at halftime. The Eagles were losing 19-16 at halftime.

"Other than their play, they were both lethargic and not into it," Coach Flannery said. "I started Kipper in the second half but didn't start Marsalis. Then Kipper was in foul trouble. He ticked me off with his attitude. Marsalis's attitude was bad, too. It was nothing disrespectful or blatant."

The people who were at the game had no idea why they weren't playing.

"It was one of those moments that as a coach I was OK with losing right now," Coach Flannery said. "I wanted to make sure to reward the guys who are playing hard with more minutes and send a message to these two guys that if we are going to be good this year we are going to need them and we are going to need them with the right attitude. If they don't have the right attitude, we aren't going to win with them or without them."

Those coming off the bench knew fully well what was going on and were ready to accept their roles of adding more minutes and doing whatever needed to be done.

"He instilled that in us freshman year," Riley said. "He would tell us that there are two freshman teams feeding into the JV team and that narrows down even more going into varsity. He doesn't care who you are or who you think you are. I don't think Marsalis played the entire second half. He wasn't playing to the coach's expectations for him. He had no problem going to the bench, saying these are the guys who are going to play well. If this guy is shooting well this game, he is going to play regardless of what he has done or didn't do in the past."

The Eagles won the game against a really good team without the two.

"That obviously sent home a bigger message because now we could beat good teams without you," Coach Flannery elaborated. "Either you buy in or you don't. This is your call. It worked out again. It was one of those moments that could have gone either way. I just said no. I was not going to ignore it and I was not going to let it go. We have too many guys on this team who put in too much work and effort. I'll play them despite the talent."

As another testament to the depth of the team, Parente came off the bench to hit two key free throws at the end as the Eagles won against 15th-ranked (nationally) Etiwanda (California) in a tight one, 43-40.

Parente, a role player who started the first game of the season, was in for most of the second half while Hamilton and Nichols sat out the game. The Eagles were up 41-40 when Parente was fouled and proceeded to make both free throws to force Etiwanda into playing for a three at the end of the game. He had just missed a shot that would have sealed the game.

"I missed the shot, a three, with about 30 seconds left," Parente said. "It was a bad shot and I got yelled at, but I made up for it when I got a steal, hit two free throws and iced the game."

Parente had also seen significant time in the loss from the previous night as a role player who could shoot the three if it was necessary.

"It was a tough role," Parente said. "Basically, if I made the shots, I was staying in and if I wasn't on, I'd come out. I just stuck with it. At practice I shot my shots."

In the game the Eagles had lost, he hit a couple shots helping to fuel the comeback.

One thing the team was beginning to learn is that it could play in any kind of game against any kind of team with any style of play.

In the game for fifth and sixth place, St. Ed's faced another team that was nationally ranked in the Alabama-based Wenonah, which as of two weeks prior to the game was 12-0. The Eagles took fifth and ran their record to 6-1 by going 3-1 in the tourney, capped off by the 89-86 win against Wenonah. Three double-figure scorers aided the team effort with Nichols scoring 25, Hamilton 22 and Ryan 10. Nichols and Vuyancih made the all-tournament team. Winning was a bonus on this trip.

"I tell parents that our No. 1 job and goal is to get closer together even if we don't win," Coach Flannery said. "We build this camaraderie and we come back better. I told them, 'You are experiencing this so enjoy it. How many of you are going to have the opportunity to get back to California? Take this time to get to know your teammates better and to come closer together.' They bought into all that."

Coupling the three wins in Cleveland with the three in California, the 6-1 start brought the Eagles to northeastern Ohio with more spring in their steps but more importantly more cohesive as a unit.

In California the Eagles had outdoor practices in December.

"I looked outside and saw 10 basketball courts in front of this beautiful mountain," Coach Flannery said. "I looked at the outdoor court and it was fairly flat and I told the guys to come on out and let's practice outside. It's another memory they will have. They were practicing outdoors in front of the mountains and they were running sprints together. It was a great experience. We beat two nationally ranked teams – Etiwanda and Wenonah. We learned a lot about ourselves."

This wound up being the third St. Ed's team to win 25 games and two of the best wins could have been Etiwanda and Wenonah.

Next up was defending state champion Mentor, another big test for the soaring Eagles.

Winning a state championship in basketball is not easy. Winning them back-to-back in Ohio is even harder. Very few have been able to pull off the latter. The last one to do it in Division I was Canton McKinley in 2005 and 2006. One has to look back to 1973 and 1974 to find the last school that had done it prior to McKinley when Elder accomplished the feat in AAA.

After their fine showing in California, the media now ranked the Eagles No. 1 in Greater Cleveland and No. 1 in Ohio. On the other hand, Mentor was just coming off a state championship in basketball. The Cardinals hoped to achieve the rare feat that McKinley and Elder had in the past.

The Cardinals would be the Eagles' top local test so far. If they could either beat the defending state champs or at least have a good showing, they would continue to get as much local attention as they had nationally. The Eagles were ranked in the top 20 in some national polls coming into the Mentor game.

While it was a while since St. Ed's had won a state title in basketball, the program had reached the regional final four times and state semifinal three times in the seven previous seasons. Coach Flannery told a story about his driving through western Ohio and hearing on the radio about a school winning its first sectional title in 20 years and thinking how St. Ed's fans could be spoiled after winning sectional and district titles year after year after year. Although it might look easy, it really is not.

"If I had never won a state championship, I'd be OK," Coach Flannery said. "I know the game enough and the history of the game enough to know what we have accomplished here. It's almost as good as it gets. We have done some great things over these last 18 years. The simple answer is, if it is so easy, who else has done it?

"Look at the history of basketball here at St. Ed's. We went 47 years of St. Ed's basketball before we went to that first final four with one district championship. Sometimes it gets pushed away because we are a private school or we get talent. It takes more than talent to be good in basketball. That will be the only thing I will be vocal about. I'm very humble in what we do, but if someone tells us what we have done is not a huge accomplishment or that we haven't turned the program around, I would have to say he is out of his mind."

In a Play-by-Play Classic showcase at Baldwin Wallace, not only did St. Ed's defeat the defending state champs, but it happened in blowout style, 91-49.

By now, people were starting to take St. Ed's seriously and the members of the team had good reason to believe that they could go all the way.

"We followed up the California trip well by blowing the defending state champs off the floor in a game that was never in question," Coach Flannery said. "People could argue that they (the Mentor Cardinals) are not as good as their championship team. They were starting to play well again and we just deflated them."

The Eagles shared the ball well again as four players reached double figures. Hamilton scored 22 while Nichols had 16 and Vuyancih 10. D.J. Funderburk came off the bench to also score 10. They did this by getting the ball inside and taking smart shots. They wasted no time in trying to counter the three-point shooting of Mentor. Hamilton was named the MVP of the game. While he thought it was a nice gesture by the coordinators of the tournament, he was already beginning to emerge as a true leader and an unselfish player.

"That means nothing," Hamilton said. "If I could, I would give it (the trophy) to the team."

Beating ranked teams from three different states in Palm Springs helped bring Hamilton to this point.

"We were able to bond more," said Hamilton. "We bonded 10 times more. We have a feel for one another."

Hamilton also had kind words about a teammate, Funderburk, who had played on the JV team as a freshman the previous year and *earned* his way on to the varsity as a sophomore.

"He's going to come; he's a really nice player," said Hamilton.

Coach Flannery commended Hamilton after this game, saying that he leads by his example and experience. Seventeen players made their way into the game with 13 scoring. They were buying into the system and embracing their roles.

"We got a lot of contributions from a lot of people," Coach Flannery said. "Nobody's worried about points or minutes or how they are playing. It shows how much closer they are coming together."

It was quite evident that the student-athletes were proving to others that they were worthy of the jersey.

Chapter 4

Mind Candy, *Toughness* and The Fist

Coach Flannery does his research to prepare his team mentally for both practices and games. Between the 2012-13 and 2013-14 seasons Coach Flannery issued a book called *Toughness* by Jay Bilas to all members of the team. He also continued using the FIST philosophy as postulated by Duke Coach Mike Krzyzewski and he utilized for the 2013-14 season a collection of inspirational quotations he called "Mind Candy."

He required *Toughness* as reading because he felt that the 2012-13 team wasn't tough enough. Neither Flannery nor Bilas thought "tough" to mean physically tough necessarily.

"The loss to North Royalton was a big upset after we had won several districts," Coach Flannery said. "The thing we did not have was toughness. We had no physical toughness and we had no mental toughness. We were a wreck. We had guys who didn't buy into one another and didn't buy into the team."

Bilas writes, "The toughest players and teammates believe in what their coaches and teammates are striving to accomplish and what they are capable of doing together as a team. Great teammates choose to commit fully to the team's goals and understand in the big picture what is required of each individual, even in the face of setbacks and tough competition."

Bilas goes on further to explain that "tough" doesn't mean bully-type tough, but defines it as more of a mental toughness than anything else.

"We did talk about it throughout the year, but the first thing that had to be understood is **that they had to get tough**," Coach Flannery said. "In the book, that toughness has nothing to do with starting a fight or being strong. Being tough is about being there for your teammates, working out in the morning, not complaining, taking a charge, setting a screen, etc."

T.J. Gallagher, a freshman coach but also the team's strength coach, took over with the workouts and made sure these guys were ready to go at 7 in the morning and to help them get tougher and stronger physically. Gallagher is also the football equipment manager. In that role, he worked alongside the strength coaches for football.

In a pre-season meeting, there were college coaches in the gym, one from the University of Wisconsin, two from D-II, but six in all.

"Two or three walked into the gym after I started talking. The team sat down in the middle of the floor and I was brought to tears because I was so disappointed at the way the season had ended last year and how the team was focusing and working in the beginning of this year," Coach Flannery said. "At one point last year I asked my son Sean what do you think happened last year? What happened to our team last year? 'Dad,' he said, 'as long as I have been around your teams, your best players were always your hardest workers. I didn't see that this year.'"

After the state championship game was over, Coach Flannery turned on his phone to view a text message from one of those coaches in the gym that day. It read, "It is amazing how far your team came. It was amazing how you got into them and what you did with them and you really got emotional with them. You won a state championship with them." It all happened by getting tougher.

"I wanted to get these guys tough and focused and we were going to meet every day before practice," Coach Flannery said. "I kept telling them that if this season turns out to be special, it will be something you will have forever. You'll remember."

Bilas goes on to explain how toughness is the antithesis of what it has lexically come to mean.

"When we talk about it, read it and think about what he is saying in the book, we all know or understand," Coach Flannery said. "We never equated the word 'toughness' to some of the things he is talking about.

Most associate toughness with macho or big bully. 'I'm tough. I am going to throw an elbow or I am going to cheap shot you.' It's the exact opposite. The weak guys are the ones who do that because they have so many insecurities."

The book brought out the following questions. Are you tough enough to go to practice and go hard every day? Are you tough enough to listen to a coach and execute it without complaining? Are you tough enough to set a screen? Get somebody open rather than being the guy who takes all the shots. Bilas has so many examples of what it means to be tough.

Coach T.J. Gallagher took care of the physical toughness, and Coach Flannery took care of the mental toughness.

"The reality is mental toughness counts," Coach Flannery said. "We had to see if they were mentally tough enough to go through this together. Those kids who don't play a lot showed toughness by practicing every single day despite not getting the same glory or exposure as those who did. They showed a tremendous amount of toughness. To do that without getting the accolades is as hard as anything the starters did. He put all that in words and the way he explained it is why the book is popular among coaches."

Although it might not have been a glamorous job at the time, the factory job Flannery had in college did provide an income, but it also taught him a lot about toughness.

"Toughness is about doing one's job and doing it the right way," Coach Flannery said. "They don't need to have physical altercations to be tough. One needs to be tough by doing the little things in the right way. One can learn about toughness by methodically sweeping floors the right way and cutting brake lines that need to be the exact measurement. Any slip of the hand could cut off my finger because I have to do it the right way. That makes me concentrate, be tough and do things the right way. I could apply that on the basketball floor. If I don't set the screen the right way, it is not going to work."

The team met for a mental session 90 percent of the time before every practice. The coach would give them what he called "mind candy," something he had learned from one of the coaches at USA Basketball.

"It gets the teammates together," Coach Flannery said. "They talk about a message. We talk about what we are going to do in practice. We have a theme for practice. Some of it was religious; some of it was not. Throughout the year we picked things up and a lot of it may just be based on where we are at that point of the season. I would find a quote somewhere to get my point across."

The first goal of mind candy is focus.

"It is to get the players' heads to focus on what we are doing now," Coach Flannery said. "They go to class and school during the day and they have their lives. A lot of teams would just go up to the gym and start practicing. I found this year to take a few minutes before practice and just talk about something and bring them into the mindset of going into practice. Maybe we need to take whatever is going on in our lives and put it aside for the next hour. It gets kids talking to one another. It gets them thinking. It was another tool to bring our team closer together."

Some of the mind candies are as follows:

If it is important to you, you will find a way. If is not important to you, you will find an excuse. – Jim Rohn

"Teens today find excuses for things -- even something as small as being on time, showing up to practice, showing up to meetings, bringing a notebook to meetings, wearing the uniform properly, or tucking one's shirt in," Coach Flannery said. "If it is important to a student-athlete, he will find a way to get it done. If there is something more important, such as playing video games, he will find the time no matter what else is going on in his life to do it. If it is important, he will be here all the time, be on time, and do what is right. If it is not important, I will hear excuses."

When he hears excuses from anybody, it is because the request wasn't that important. They are making up an excuse to get out of doing what they were supposed to be doing. On the other hand, when the student-athletes understand this mind candy and talk to one another about its meaning, they all tend to agree on its message and importance, and subsequently act upon it.

"They say if this is what we want to do and this is important, let's do it," Coach Flannery said. "Otherwise, we don't hear about it. I understand that some unexpected things happen, but if it happens all the time or three days a week, he is just making excuses. Then it is not that important to him. If student-athletes know that concept, they will say, 'This is what I want to do; I will do whatever I can to make it happen.' When they hear their teammates making excuses, they hold one another accountable. Quit making excuses. If this is important to you, get it done."

Yesterday is history, tomorrow is a mystery and today is a gift, which is why it is called the present. – Alice Morse Earle

"We can control what happens in front of us," Coach Flannery said. "We can only control the present. Whatever happened yesterday (didn't play well or I had a bad day) and if things weren't going well, it is over. What we do today is going to affect tomorrow and down the road. We can't do anything about that either. We can only control what happens now. It's God's gift to us. He is giving us another day to live on this earth. One needs to be in the moment when it comes to being a better player or a better person."

Your comfort zone is your enemy. – Unknown

"When comfortable, we get lazy and complacent and tend to be satisfied," Coach Flannery explained. "When we are sore and tired or things aren't going well, we learn a lot about ourselves. When we are comfortable, we tend to relax. Driving ourselves from our comfort zones is how we get better. We improve by making mistakes and pushing ourselves. We get better by learning about ourselves and by failing. It's the old cliché` of having to fail in order to appreciate winning. Get out of the comfort zone in order to push ourselves to become better as people and players. Don't feel too comfortable sitting in class and failing to pay attention, because that is staying in one's comfort zone."

Don't give up fast because of how far you have to go. Instead consider how far you've come. – Unknown

"It's a lesson in patience and perseverance," Coach Flannery said. "It's because it looks so far that people stop. 'It's too far, it's too long, and it's too much,' they say. 'We want to win a state championship, but it is so far away. We have to get to practice every day. We have to work out every day. We have to get bigger and stronger. It is so far away. Forget it. It is too much work.' When they think this way, we have to make them realize at what they have done in the past to earn this opportunity. The skill level and gifts from God and all the hard work that we put in up to this point have brought us to this moment. We are a lot closer than we think. Don't let that go to waste. Understand that we are close any time during the season. We are only a couple weeks (later in the season) and a couple months (early in the season) from achieving the ultimate goal. Let's not forget about all the hard work that was put into it."

When the eyes say one thing and tongue something else, believe the former. – Ralph Waldo Emerson

"That went to our body language on the floor," Coach Flannery said. "A player could tell me he is doing as instructed and tell me he is playing as hard as he is playing on the floor, but I could see whether it is true or not. I could see what is going on. My eyes are not lying. Quit trying to talk your way through a lot of things. Quit making excuses. It is not what you say, but how you act in the end. That goes for off the floor too. How is he acting? What does his body language say? Quit talking a good game and start playing it. We don't want lip service; we want production."

You might have the will to win but do you have the will to prepare to win? – Unknown

"Everyone wants to be successful and win, but not everybody wants to do the little things it takes to win," Coach Flannery said. "It is getting up early in the morning and getting in the weight room and spending extra time after practice and working on one's game. That's listening to coaches and teammates and doing the right things in the classroom to stay eligible and play. So many people talk a good game. They want to win, but the reality is the numbers decline when it comes to putting in the effort to prepare to win. As coaches, we take that into account with scouting and making sure we understand our opponent. We have to understand that we are putting our teams in a position to win, so are we preparing in practice to win? Preparation is more important than the game. The ones who put the time and preparation into achieving their goals are the more successful."

A diamond is coal under pressure. – Henry Kissinger

"As with a diamond, we make ourselves successful by putting ourselves in tough situations," Coach Flannery said. "There might be some failures. The greatest players in history are the ones who did well under pressure. That's what separates a diamond from a piece of coal. A diamond is great because it's shiny and stands out and thrives in those big moments. The stars step up when the big time comes."

If you fail to prepare, you're prepared to fail. – Vince Lombardi

"If you don't put time and effort into achieving a goal, you are setting yourself up for failure," Coach Flannery said. "Do you want to talk about achieving a goal or are you going to put the time and effort into it to get the end result? One of my biggest fears after a loss is that I look at my team and determine that we lost because I didn't prepare them to win. If I don't prepare them to win, I am preparing them to lose. That fear drives me as a coach. I never want to look at my team and say, 'I'm the reason you lost, because I didn't get you ready.' There have been many times after games when I have said that I could have done more prep in practice or before the game to get us a victory."

Persistence is pushing the self through not forward to exceed limitations. -- Unknown

"The whole point is that persistence is pushing and pushing and pushing until one gets what he wants," Coach Flannery said. "Mike

Brown, a former NBA coach, had a saying about hitting the rock -- chipping a rock one hit at a time. It's like the diamond theory. If we hit that rock as many times as we can, eventually it will break and eventually it will turn into what we want. It is not going to take one hit to break it down or make it what we want it to be (Bilas said getting to the top of a ladder in one step is not going to happen, but getting down to the bottom of the ladder in one step is possible). One can't get it in one swing. We have to be consistent. We have to keep pushing forward and through every adversity there is and go on and on and on. It takes time and persistence to accomplish it."

You are never as good as you think you are or as bad as you think you are, but you are never far from either. – Brad Stevens

"It is up to the individual to choose which way he is going to go," Coach Flannery said. "If we think things are bad, they are never as bad as we make them out to be. They might seem bad to us, but people looking in from the outside might not see them as being that bad. When having success and doing well, we might feel good about ourselves, but we might not be as good as we think we are. The reality is that we are not far from either one on any given day. As a basketball team, if we think we are really good, we are not far away from being bad if we are not playing well. Listen, this whole thing could change on any given day."

The players found that the mind candy would get them ready for practice and they would have better practices as a result.

"Regardless of what everyone did in practice that day, it put everyone in the same mindset; the mind candy got everyone focused and ready to go," Riley said. "This is what we have to do in practice. This is what we have to do to get better every day. It was the common goal. Whatever the mind candy was for that day, it would put into perspective what we needed to achieve that day or what we needed to do at that point of the season. We communicated better on and off the floor this year than we did last year. The mind candy would work because we would go down there and talk about what we thought the mind candies were saying, what they meant and how they applied to us and to our teammates at that point."

With the Bilas book in mind, the mind candy helped the players get mentally tough for practice.

"They just gave us a good mindset once we came into practice," Pisco said. "We were always able to understand what needed to be done and the mind candy helped understand what was going on for our team every week. It was perfect for us and something we could relate to."

Some of the players used them for support.

"They made me think," Walters said. "They were a support especially the ones about finding a way. Some of them were really powerful. It made us look at things differently. We didn't want to be a team that made excuses. When it came to practice every day it got us to go hard. As good as they were, by themselves they helped us see things from a different perspective."

The mind candy helped bring the players together as a team. They were able to get the players ready to combine the physical part of the game with the mental part of it. The mind candies' inspiration would eventually show up in the state championship game.

"Those things may seem little and we might just sit in there and listen," Tony Vuyancih said, "but I'm a big believer in if I keep being told it, it becomes true. If it is in the front of my mind, that's what I am going to do. We kept being told these things at state. It kept our goal in mind. The mind candies told us how we were going to achieve that goal besides going every day to practice just to practice. We were doing more to become better players. It wasn't just working on our skills. We were working on our mental games."

In addition to the Mind Candy and Toughness was the FIST that Flannery began introducing for the 2001-02 season after Coach Krzyzewski published a book titled *Five Point Play* about Duke's championship season from the previous year.

"I don't think there was ever a moment when I said, OK this is it," Coach Flannery said. "After those three really good years and three tough years, I was looking for that thing that would separate us from other teams and other programs. The 2001-2002 year was when my philosophy as a coach began to change. We were going to spend more time on other things outside of basketball. It was a Mike Krzyzewski book that I read that got me going. We came close together with the FIST, which came from his book. Each finger stood for something: 1) pride, 2) communication, 3) collective responsibility, 4) caring and 5) trust. As we kept building on those five things; we kept coming closer and closer together as a team. I bought into that and I sold my guys into that. I thought that once they bought into those things, we became a very good basketball team despite not being as talented as some of the teams we had had in the past."

In 2002, it was fresh and it was new. Krzyzewski said that the philosophy behind the FIST is that with an open hand a team can't do much. Instead, it's one finger at a time coming together to form a fist. The fingers coming closer and tighter together as we make this fist is much like a team creating togetherness as each player pulls closer and tighter to all the others. A fist is much stronger than an open hand. A team is stronger than its loosened individual parts.

"He talked about caring for one another, caring for our teammates, caring for our coaches, caring for other people," Coach Flannery said. "Being on a boys' basketball team, some guys might have thought that wasn't necessarily a macho thing to do. Our talking about it meant a lot to the players. It was OK to care for one another. It was OK to show some emotion. They were OK with that. If we are going to build a team and if it is going to be a strong team, it is going to have to be like a family. We have to care for one another. It might not always be great, but we care when things are going well or not so well on and off the court."

Then there was communication.

"Communication is huge in the game of basketball and most sports," Coach Flannery said. "It is important to communicate with teammates by letting them know what we are doing on the floor. If a screen is coming, we have to know to yell and talk. If a substitute comes in, a teammate has to know which opponent is that sub to be matched against. We have to get guys to talk to one another, and that builds off the floor too. Student-athletes who are talking to one another off the floor start building relationships."

Also there was pride. It was like the Worthy of the Jersey theme of the 2013-14. It was selling the program.

"It was the pride of putting on a St. Ed's uniform, the pride of making the team, the pride of being something bigger than oneself," Coach Flannery said.

The fourth was collective responsibility.

"We've talked about these things consistently every year since then," Coach Flannery said. "Collective responsibility is simply everyone takes responsibility for what goes on. If one person makes the shot, we all make the shot. If one person takes a charge on defense, we all take a charge on defense. To get anyone to buy into that is really hard; to get teenagers to buy into that is even harder. Even if they begin to talk that way, they are only hearing what we are saying and repeating it. At first they make fun of it. If he makes a shot, they all say, 'We made that shot or I made that shot.' That's when it starts and it builds from that. They start believing it. They start understanding that the one who made the pass is as important as the one making the shot. 'If I set a screen to get that guy open, he wouldn't have been open if I hadn't set the screen.' If all of them buy into that, they realize that they need one another in order to score points, and they need to do different things. Collective responsibility came into it on and off the court. When somebody makes a mistake, we all make a mistake."

The fifth thing was trust.

"The way we build trust is by telling the truth," Coach Flannery said. "We tell student-athletes this is why they are not playing. This is what you need to do to get better. This is why you are good. We compliment them when they are supposed to be complimented, but we also tell them the truth. We don't bring them down. We don't criticize them, but we let them know. We are honest with them and tell them like it is.

"I expect that back from them. Once we build that trust with the student-athletes, they trust us a lot more and they understand. They know we are not lying to them, and we are just trying to make a successful season happen. When putting all those things together, a team can make something great out of its season."

So if a student-athlete could learn from the mind candy, become mentally tough at the roughest times and focus on the five elements of the FIST, he could be well on his way to becoming "worthy of the jersey."

Chapter 5

The Holy Cross Philosophy

While becoming tougher, learning from mind candy and buying into the FIST are three mental components that bring members of a team to a point of being worthy of the jersey, there is a fundamental philosophy at the school that makes student-athletes sufficiently strong both mentally and spiritually to have the makings of a championship team.

Established in 1949, St. Edward High School was founded by the Brothers of Holy Cross, who had come from the University of Notre Dame in South Bend, Indiana to provide an alternative to the long-established Jesuit school, St. Ignatius.

While a boy does not have to be Catholic to attend St. Edward, most of the students are. The Holy Cross and Catholic philosophies help mold the well-rounded young man. When he has the academic, athletic, and spiritual parts all together, he can set off for college as an already sound individual.

The Brothers of Holy Cross Web site states:

> The Brothers of Holy Cross are members of an international congregation of Catholic religious brothers and priests who lead extraordinary lives by bringing hope to others. Devoted to God through our ministry and prayer, we strive to make a difference in the world by being present and available to the people and communities we serve.

> Although ministry is essential to the life of a brother, it does not define our life. Rather, it is our lifestyle that makes us unique — we take this extraordinary journey of faith *together.* Abroad or at home, Brothers of Holy Cross live in community. In good times or challenging times, we can always count on our fellow brothers for support and encouragement.

The word "together" was emphasized for a reason. It would play out throughout the championship season and is the backbone of the St. Edward philosophy.

"We get students from various backgrounds and not everybody is Catholic although the majority is," Coach Flannery said. "It is the school's religion and philosophy. It is part of our makeup and part of what we try to instill in our students. I am not going to pound it into my players that they have to believe this way. We are going to talk about being Catholic and being at a Holy Cross school and what that means. It is about attitude, effort, and the person rather than the God of worship."

For St. Ed's basketball, the Holy Cross philosophy is more about representing one's school and family. They use the Holy Cross examples to help guide the young men to try to make good decisions and to try to be good people.

"That's the way I approach it whether it is a quote from the Bible or the fear of God as the ultimate punishment if someone doesn't behave or do well as we Catholics strive to do," Coach Flannery said. "We use some of that to instill some of the values and virtues into our players. We try to teach them how to act and how to behave as members of a Holy Cross school."

The team does have prayer services and is certain to pray before every pre-game meal and after every game in the locker room. They did have a season-opening Mass. They try to incorporate that part of their Catholicism into the team as more of a general guideline.

"We talk about servant leadership here at St. Ed's," Coach Flannery said. "That's what we are founded upon. We are not just about helping those who are doing well but helping anyone."

Archbishop Edward Francis Hoban, while he was still the Bishop of Cleveland before becoming an archbishop, helped found St. Edward in the late 1940s. He wanted to have a school that would appeal to the common man, the sons of laborers, boilermakers, welders, mechanics, firemen, truck drivers as well as those who came from more affluent backgrounds.

Flannery drew from the Holy Cross and Catholic philosophies to inspire his team for the championship game against Upper Arlington. He read this quote from Deuteronomy in the Old Testament:

> *"Be strong and courageous. Do not be afraid or terrified because of them, for the Lord your God goes with you; he will never leave you nor forsake you."*
>
> – Deuteronomy 31:6

"It was inspired by God," Coach Flannery said. "That was our way of getting the spiritual part of it. The players had to understand that this was important."

Most of the mind-candy quotes Coach Flannery had used to instill the consistent message were from various coaches and other leaders, but for the state title game, he used the Bible.

"I thought it would be appropriate since it was the state championship and the last time we were going to be together," Coach Flannery said. "The first time we gathered was a Mass. The last time we assemble should be something from the Bible. We are going to face some adversity. We need to hold strong. We have to understand the big picture. I know it doesn't feel like that right now, but this is just a game, I told them. It's the most important thing to you (the players) right now. In the big picture of things, school's really important, God's really important, and family's really important. How do I as a coach try to send that message here? These student-athletes are going into probably the biggest game of their lives. How do I try to keep that in perspective? I thought it was appropriate for the time to keep them grounded."

In jest, it was a long-held belief that when Notre Dame's football team would play, God was on the side of the Irish and was why they had had so much success over the years.

"I never believed that," Coach Flannery said. "I am a religious guy, but I never believed that God is on my side against other people. I always ask for help to make sure we stay healthy and to play to the best of our abilities. That's all I can ask for. If my team goes out there and plays great, everything else takes care of itself. If God is up there watching St. Ed's play any given opponent, it never crosses my mind that He might be rooting for St. Ed's. I do think it is important to have faith. We have faith in ourselves and in what we are doing and we have faith in one another. They have to have faith in their teammates.

"That is what God looks for. He looks for people who are genuine good people, who are looking out for other people. We're happy for the people who won and we console our teammates. If we win, we do it the right way and have to understand that those guys on the other side are hurting. We don't get in their faces. We celebrate and enjoy it, but we have to respect the opponent."

Everything the school and basketball program does is faith-based whether they preach it or not. That's the way coaches live their lives as the example.

"If I am telling these young men to do one thing, then I have to walk away doing the same thing," Coach Flannery said. "Our job is to be mentors to these boys and win basketball games. We teach kids to do things the right way. We preach that by saying the right things."

It is all reflected in the way someone is respected.

"They are not going to respect a student-athlete for scoring 30 points," Coach Flannery said. "They may respect him for a moment, but they are going to respect him more for who he is as a person. How he treats other people and how he acted on the floor and how he represented the school and himself and his family gains more respect.

"It is not all about winning and losing; it is all about what impact I had on kids. I know what coaches mean when they say the relationships are way more important than winning and losing. When former players walk back to this office after they are done playing here, they sit down and thank me for what I did. That's when the real prize comes in."

Another part of being worthy of the jersey is living the Holy Cross philosophy in the right way.

Chapter 6

Worthiness Means No. 18 Counts as Much as No. 1

Since Coach Flannery assumed the top job in the St. Edward basketball program, there have been few teams that have had what is considered a "superstar," someone who does a large chunk of the scoring. Yes, the 1997-98 team had enough talent that some of them went on to the pros and were a large part of the reason for that championship, but in most cases during Flannery's 18 years St. Ed's has not had that one scorer to carry the load.

There is a reason for this. The system calls for every player to be a contributor – from the five starters all the way down to player No. 15, or in the case of the 2013-14 team, all the way down to player No. 18. Being a good teammate and good practice player counts for as much as being the one to score all the points and play all the minutes. This is a philosophy Coach Flannery tries to get his players to buy into every year.

It might be cliché to say that only if the team believes in accomplishing great things and each member of the team sacrifices for one another will great things happen. Many teams have had all the right pieces, got along well, and created a great deal of synergy, but their results were short of the goals.

As a coach, there are two paths one might take to win. One is to go with talented individuals and hope to have the higher number of superstars. The other is to go with good talent – but not "superstar" talent

– and together each player works better as part of a team than as an individual.

When the late Herb Brooks was named the head coach of the 1980 U.S. Olympic hockey team, he put together a roster of players, not of the best individual talent but of young men he thought would be the best team players who would work as a unit. He didn't want a group of superstars going every which way; he wanted everyone on the same page. Those on the committee were appalled by his selection. In the previous Olympics the U.S. team had been mauled. They were given little chance to win a game, let alone beat the vaunted Soviets or win a medal. Yet, they defied all odds, upset the Soviets in the semifinal game and went on to win the gold medal.

Miracle, a movie about the hockey team that included St. Edward alumnus Todd Harkins as one of the actors, had a scene in it in which Coach Brooks wanted to emphasize how important it is to be a team player. After a tough practice when he thought some of the players were acting selfishly, he had the players skate from the goal line to the blue line, back and forth several times. The young men kept skating on and on and on. Coach Brooks would say when they would complete a skate to the line, "again." He would repeat "again" over and over again as the legs of the players continued to feel more like lead every second. In the scene, the janitor to the building was ready to turn off the lights and go home, but Coach Brooks kept them skating in the dark. Finally, at one moment, team member Mike Eruzione, got down on his knees and shouted to the ceiling, "My name is Mike Eruzione and I play for the United States of America." That's all Coach Brooks needed to hear. He nodded and ended the practice right there and sent the boys home.

Nothing irks Coach Flannery more than when a player has an individual agenda and is not acting in a way that benefits the team. Only when all members of the team are working toward that common goal and doing only things necessary to accomplish that goal will great things happen.

"We want them to experience the good and the bad," Coach Flannery said. "Winning the state championship makes everything better. Everybody is on cloud nine. Guys walk away with a feeling of success. We don't ever want them walking away without that feeling. The previous year they lost in the district championship, but if they walk away with a better understanding of how to be successful and how to do things, good or bad, then there is still a sense of success."

It takes hard work to win, but it takes more team work than hard work to win championships

"I think most of the guys get that out of it," Coach Flannery said. "They realize that they need hard work just to be a part of it. I get a chuckle out of a parent who would call me and say, 'My son works hard. He is in the weight room and the gym and he puts all this time and effort into it. Why doesn't he play more? Why doesn't he get more attention?' They always use the excuse that 'my son works so hard,' and my response is that that is why he is at where he is at right now. All that hard work and dedication put him into the position he is in now."

What happens beyond that is out of anyone's control. Maybe he is not as talented as others to play much, but it is still his job to be an ideal teammate and do whatever it takes to make the team better.

"Because he works hard is why he is on the team," Coach Flannery went on. "That's what separates him from everybody else. Everyone at this level is working hard. Some are more talented than others. We just hope that the hard work pays off and that each can be successful and a part of something big. It's not all about playing time, shooting baskets and scoring points."

One sign of a great team player is whether he is willing to take ownership of whatever happens and be accountable. As a captain, Hamilton learned this throughout the season. He realized that by taking the hit for things not going well, he would help the team more than he would by scoring a lot of points, taking a lot of shots or getting triple doubles.

Much of this teamwork combined with hard work and accountability starts at the top.

"I always hate taking credit as a coach, but in a sense it starts there," Coach Flannery said. "What I allow them to get away with and what I stand up to is crucial. There have been years when I've wavered, when I have let some things go. It might be small, but it becomes a bigger problem.

"If guy No. 13 who doesn't play much doesn't get away with something and guy No. 1 or No. 2 does because they are guy one or two, they (the ones on the second or third string) see that and become a problem. They see that this isn't fair. They become disappointed or disinterested. We can lose guys one by one. I think as a coach it starts putting a message into their heads."

Once in their heads, the message must manifest itself through the players.

"At some point it is only effective if players buy into my philosophy of every player counting equally and take ownership," Coach Flannery said. "This team took ownership. Tony was the vocal leader and he kept constantly getting on his teammates about doing things the right way and when they screwed up to come back. Tony had some player only meetings. When we have that, I know they are hearing my message. They are starting to buy into the program."

Coach Flannery realizes that he can never control what everybody is thinking, but when student-athletes are showing that they are buying into his philosophy, they are following the rules and know what is going on, he knows he has something special.

"When I as a coach don't have to say it any more because they are saying it, that's when I know I have them," Coach Flannery said. "Winning a state championship at that point to me is not as big as their buying into it no matter how far they go. If and when they lose along the way, those players are the ones who take the blame. They say, 'We didn't do this or that, and that's why we lost.' They don't say 'You didn't do this or you didn't do that or coach didn't do that.' They take ownership of the team and what they are doing. I saw that time and time again with the 2014 team."

Given a choice between playing a lot and being on a state championship team, any true team player and good teammate would select the latter.

"On this team (2013-14) I would be floored if there were one player who said I would have rather played more than how the season played out," Coach Flannery said. "Up and down, when we look at every single student-athlete individually, whether it is guy one or guy 18, they are all OK with how it played out. Maybe a little during the season we see some of that because no one knows how it is going to end. My approach is that I tell the guys at the beginning of the season what their role probably will be.

"I ask them, 'Are you OK with that?' If they have any hesitation, then I tell them don't play. Definitely going into the season they know what their role will be. I've had plenty of guys over the years look me in the eye and tell me, 'I am going to be OK; I just want to be on the team' and it turns into a nightmare. Some of that is parent-driven. Sometimes a student thought he was just going to get on the team and work his way up to play. It doesn't happen and so he becomes upset. When I get those guys, even when they are not playing in the game, it hurts the whole team. They'll bring the other guys down. That just wasn't the case with this state championship team. There is that whole saying that a team is only as good as its weakest player or its weakest link. That's the truth. It's not about skill. It's about how each person is as a teammate. If guy 15 is disruptive, it makes everyone else disruptive and it starts spreading. If he's saying, 'I don't like this or I don't like the coach or I don't like this guy or that guy,' it starts spreading throughout the locker room. It damages everybody."

Coach Flan would not be floored about what was said by Connor Pisco, who was in that 11-to-18 group of players.

"I was perfectly fine with not playing this year," said Pisco, whose brother, Kyle, played college ball at John Carroll after St. Ed's. "Everyone has to be comfortable with his role. It's something everyone fell into. I fit in perfectly this year. It's always nice to play, but to be on a team as good as we were, it is just as good. There's nothing that could replace that feeling. Coming in, everyone's goal was to win a state championship, but what we didn't realize was how much work and effort it took to winning one. It was something we all dreamed of, but the time we put in and the dedication we had really paid off in the long run. Going off that, for the guys who weren't playing, if we got on players who were playing, they would always listen to what we had to say. That was for the best. They understood that we were watching everything that they did. They were able to correct that and turn it into a positive."

The 1998 team had taken ownership for whatever happened and functioned as good teammates with the end result being a state championship. The 2013-14 team had a similar mind set and a similar group of guys.

Ansberry, a long-time assistant to Flannery, was a member of the 1998 championship team.

"If someone is sitting and not playing and is yet very happy, it means one of two things," Coach Ansberry said. "Either he is one of the greatest persons you ever want to meet, or someone who has put on a front. Guys might not be playing, but I could tell whether they are into the game or not. I could see them thinking, 'Man, I really want to get in there.' Those are the types that we want. They are ready and they are pushing the starters. They are not just, 'OK, I am not going to play' kind of thing. That's (ones eager to get in and aiding the starters) what I started to see in this team."

It all comes down to not only being a team player but also being a good role player. It is a matter of understanding one's role and living that role as the season plays out, no matter what the outcome or one's personal feelings.

"The roles started to develop to which we had the starting five and we had Will, Pat, Darien and D.J. and those guys," Coach Ansberry said. "We had great individuals like Pisco, Jack Flannery and Parente and those guys that reminded me a lot of some of the guys from the '98 team like me, Nick Barile, and other guys who were just there to push and knew their roles. They weren't going to push the issue, coming in every two weeks asking what they could do to get playing time."

Being a role player and sacrificing for the team so that he could have great things happen, like winning a championship down the line, starts with a student-athlete's acceptance of his role. However, he must also realize that sometimes it takes more than just accepting it.

"It's not just accepting, but it is *embracing* the role," said Josh Nugent, the head JV coach, who coached many of the players on the team during their development years. "With 18 guys, it was very unique. At some point there comes the realization of who you are within the team. There's two different ways someone can go with that. He could be the guy who pouts and brings the negative energy in, which could quite honestly in talking about the importance of the bench, tear a team apart. We could have those bottom guys that might not play as much start to mope, or they can embrace it."

It goes back to the trust factor that Coach Flannery expects from his players and coaching staff.

"We build trust with the players; we say this will be their roles right now," Coach Nugent said. "We make sure they are OK with it. If they are not, they are not going to be on this team. They will be distractions if they don't leave. If someone doesn't accept his role, that means he doesn't want to be here. If he JUST accepts it, then it is OK, that's it and 'I am done with it. I'm no longer going to compete. I am no longer going to push myself or my teammates because I am the 15th guy and nothing is going to change.' Well, if someone *embraces* it and says he is the 15th guy on the team, there is still a chance he could move up and a chance he could help this team and he is going to be the best 15th man that there is. He's going to help his team in his role: that's *embracing* it."

It generally takes a good half year. Always at the beginning of the year, everybody thinks he can and will play.

"We love that," Coach Nugent said. "That's what we want because they are competitive. They want to be out there and they want to help. At some point there is some realization of 'I am not going to play as much, but I have to be ready when I get called. It might not be as often as I would like.' Our guys embraced it and understood that they could affect a game."

By the end of the season, the 2013-14 team had become well known because of its depth and how much each member of the team contributed. The guys in the student section of the cheering crowd picked up on it and had T-shirts printed up that said "Bench Mob."

"We had unwavering support from the guys in the crowd. Any time we would look over and see that the guys were in it and supporting us and getting on the other team," Coach Nugent said. "We had those guys coming in and knowing what they needed to do. They were playing within themselves. It was Pat Riley coming in and controlling the game with his tempo, controlling the game defensively and offensively. Another thing was Will Meyer being in the right place at the right time. It was Darien Knowles coming in and being that spark and not trying to do too much. Phil Parente knew when he was coming in that he was coming in for one reason and one reason only – to get an open look and to get a shot. Guys started to understand that. Whether they were starters or not didn't matter; they were right there. It was, 'Here's what I need to do individually to make this thing work.'"

Riley, a sixth and seventh man, was able to get introspection from the others down the bench. That team effort would be the driving factor throughout the season.

"Anyone who comes to St. Ed's could have gone to his local high school and been an all-star there, but I'd rather be in a program that has the storied tradition of St. Ed's," Riley said. "It's more special because students are coming from all over the place. That being said, these student-athletes knew they could have started and played somewhere else. Obviously they are good basketball players and have good basketball knowledge. Coming off the floor and sitting down on the bench, I would have someone like Connor telling me that this is what this guy is doing and look for that. When I would come back to the bench, there would always be someone telling me good job and helping me improve with something I was doing out there. It would usually be something I wouldn't see."

The starters bought into it as well.

"Guys were getting on each other," Coach Flannery said. "I saw the biggest maturation with Kipper (Nichols). Did he fall off the train and still act immature? Yes, but Kipper in team meetings and in practices began getting on other players about how to act and how to play and to get focused. When my best player is doing that and buying into that and starting to grow, I know we are starting to become really good.

"They could have taken the ownership the other way – talking bad and going against the coaches and start questioning what I am doing. When they start buying into the program the right way and sending the same message I am sending, it becomes easy for the coach. It is also part of that recipe of winning a state championship. What I need is for the guys to be the leaders – on and off the court."

While those on the third and fourth strings might have found it hard to accept their roles by supporting the players who were getting the minutes and scoring the points, those who were getting the playing time also had to supportive of the guys who were supportive of them.

"They (the top players) brought everyone in," Coach Ansberry said. "They didn't treat them like, 'You guys aren't playing; you're just scrubs.' Easily, that could have happened this year. With 18 guys on the team, Marsalis or Kipper could have been talking to an 18th guy and said, 'I am not talking to you,' one of those deals like, 'I don't even know how you are on the team,' type of deal. They could have had that attitude but they didn't. That comes from the head coach, who was building that type of atmosphere."

A starter has to make a third and fourth-string student-athlete feel as if he is wanted, that he is valuable and that how the starter plays is a direct reflection of how supportive others on the bench have been.

"They pushed and encouraged those guys to work hard in practice," Coach Flannery said. "When we watched these guys in the off season, these guys who knew they were not going to play much worked just as hard as anybody else if not harder. When the first group of guys sees that, it pushes them more to work hard. He should be thinking, 'Why should this guy be out-working me when he is not even going to be playing or playing as many minutes as I am?' So we have that relationship of that top-tier and bottom-tier pushing each other. They work but they respect one another with what they are doing both on and off the court. We need that relationship and that goes back to team building. When building a team, the bottom guys have to buy in, but the top guys also have to buy in and make them a part of it."

The players understood the difference between the previous year's team that might have had talent and the championship team that had the team concept sewn together.

"With the competition we played, we had to be a good basketball team," junior Kipper Nichols said. "A lot of people want winners. At that next level, everybody could score. That's a lot of the things Coach Flan talked about, how it is on me and I have to do a lot of different things. Last year we had the talent to win the state championship, but we didn't have the team to do it. Coach Flan really emphasized us playing together as a team this year. Marsalis sacrificed showing what he could do as a player throughout the game. He (prior to the 2013-14 season) was a victim of that concept (of individuality). Certain sacrifices and doing things we are not used to doing all came into play."

The mindset of sacrificing for the team emanated from the pre-season meetings with each individual player.

"We all had meetings with Coach Flan at the beginning of the year and he basically asked me the question," Parente said. "What if I fall into a role where I am not playing a lot? I told him I would be happy just to be on the team and be able to help out any way I could, helping out players in practice so that we could win a state championship. That was our goal. I didn't care about how much I played or how much I didn't play. It was more about just winning."

Once everyone is on the same page about being a good teammate, from one to 18 and 18 to one, the coaching and talent could take over and do what it had to do to win a championship.

"We need to have it; a team is not going to win with guys who can't execute what I do as a coach," Coach Flannery said. "The ingredient to have a state championship team does start with talent. Right up there with talent is molding that talent together to play well as a team, unselfishly and hard. If we could get everyone on that team to buy into that one goal, that's when we have success. Even if we don't win a state championship, we have the ingredients to win a state championship. When guys come in and they don't worry about just scoring or what their stat line is and are simply worried about playing basketball at any cost, that's when we have a championship team. We have to realize that they are going to get selfish and they correct themselves."

So it went. From fourth string to first string and down the roster from first string to fourth string, in the end it was more of a horizontal line than a vertical line, with each component equally as significant as the other in a quest to become "worthy of the jersey."

Chapter 7

Worthy of the Winning Streak

While Marsalis Hamilton began demonstrating some leadership on the California trip and in the Mentor triumph, he was only one of four captains on the 2013-14 club.

The captain crew was made up of four seniors -- three starters, and, because depth would be a central part of this team, one second teamer. Hamilton was joined by Vuyancih, Walters, and Riley. Vuyancih had been a captain as a junior in 2012-13.

“I thought going into this season what was going to be important was picking the captains,” Coach Flannery said. “The previous year the leadership wasn’t that great. Some of the players took back-seat roles on purpose and didn’t step up as leaders. We had to pick guys their teammates respected. Vuyancih remained a vocal leader through the end of his high school career.

“We always look at our best player, our most-rounded player, who people just respect because of his ability to play and Marsalis was that guy for us this year. If he didn’t embrace it or he showed off or didn’t do what he was supposed to do, that would have really hurt the team this year. He took strides and became a good leader.”

Then there was Walters.

“The point guard should be one of the captains,” Coach Flannery said. “He’s the leader on the floor and he’s the coach on the floor. He had to change positions and was trying to be the vocal leader of the team. My sign of support to him was that people have to listen to him as a leader."

Then there was the Bench Mob as they came to be known. They needed a leader, too.

"With this year's team having so many guys, 18, it was important to have a captain on the bench," Coach Flannery said. "I knew at the beginning of the season that Malcolm and Pat were going to share the point-guard duty. What if Pat would have ended up earning more minutes than Malcolm as the season went on and now my captain is sitting on the bench?"

With their first road game in the Cleveland area approaching since the John Adams game, the Eagles were going to need the leadership to take on several ranked teams on their own home courts.

For the 7-1 Eagles, the next stop was again on the East Side against Beachwood. Although a smaller school, Beachwood had one of the best overall teams in the Cleveland area.

The No. 1-ranked Eagles carbon copied what they had already done a few times this season, jumping all over the opponent from the opening gun. Against the Bison, it was 12-0 before the hosts knew what had hit them.

It all started with Hamilton tossing an alley-oop pass a few seconds into the game that Walters leaped high for to stick in the basket.

"We were moving the ball around, we were getting the ball inside, and we were attacking the rim," Coach Flannery said after the game. "The game could have been over by halftime."

As it was, the Eagles held a 19-point halftime lead, 45-26, after leading by as many as 20 points in the first half.

Two trends were becoming evident, one encouraging and one not. The high number of baskets scored by the Eagles that were assisted was definitely a positive. The play opening the game set the tone for this.

The fact that Beachwood nearly got back into this game, cutting the score down to 10 points, 69-59, was a drawback.

Allowing the opponent back into the game presented a wake-up call and learning experience. It also prompted the captains to emerge as leaders and for the team to take ownership of its mistakes.

"I like to have experiences like this," Coach Flannery said after the game. "We can use it as teaching points. Winning by 40 or 50 is nice, but it is also nice to have some tough situations."

Funderburk, only a sophomore, came off the bench to score 17 points. Nichols ended with 20 points. Hamilton had 18.

Next up was St. Edward arch-rival St. Ignatius for the first of two regular-season games against the Wildcats.

Defeating St. Ignatius in any sport at any time at any level (freshman, JV, varsity, club) is almost like a double victory for St. Edward. St. Edward beating St. Ignatius twice in a season in any sport is quite a feat and is cherished by St. Edward alumni, students and fans alike.

In football, the St. Edward-St. Ignatius annual battle has been ranked by Rivals.com as the sixth greatest high school football rivalry in the country.

The Eagles and Wildcats played each other in football only a few times in the 1950s. The two schools did not meet in football between 1958 and 1970. The rivalry was revised in 1971. By the '70s it became an annual occurrence. St. Ed's controlled the series in the 1970s and early-to-mid '80s, but St. Ignatius, on its way to 11 state championships, has controlled the series from the late '80s to the present. In fact, the only loss suffered by St. Ed's during the regular season in 2013 was to St. Ignatius in First Federal Lakewood Stadium. Such dominance by St. Ignatius in football leaves St. Ed's fans looking toward their other teams such as basketball to compensate.

The ice-hockey rivalry between St. Ed's and St. Ignatius has also become a fierce one over the years. They have played in front of more than 3,000 fans in the Gund Arena. In the district championship game (2009) the two teams went to six overtimes before the Eagles finally won. In 2012, St. Ignatius went into the district championship game with a 39-0 record before losing to the Eagles.

St. Edward and the Cats have also met in state championship games in basketball, baseball and rugby.

Usually, the basketball battle between the Eagles and Cats is sold out with 2,000 fans attending (sometimes more depending upon the venue) whether it is played in Sullivan Gymnasium or the Eagles' Nest. This year would be no different.

The January 18, 2014 game against the Cats would be the first official home game for the Eagles since December 21.

Up to this point, the Eagles had been building big leads on their opponents, using their defense to generate quick points and offensively pounding the ball inside. Coach Flannery said after the California trip that this team was capable of adapting to any style of play. For sure, St. Ignatius Head Coach Sean O'Toole would break out something to throttle the Eagles. Ranked No. 1 in the Greater Cleveland metropolitan area and Ohio and No. 19 in the nation by the media, the Eagles were expecting a close game, much like those they had experienced in California.

Regardless of records, this semiannual battle brings out the best in the student-athletes involved both physically and emotionally. This game is also one in which the student cheering section plays a big factor.

The Wildcats were thinking upset from the start, opening up a 4-0 lead.

Throughout most of the first three quarters, the Cats would be able to stay in the game even though St. Ed's held the lead most of the night. Funderburk dropped in a bucket off a lofty pass by Nichols to make it a 19-point game, 42-23, shortly before the end of the third quarter. Depth played a factor in the Eagles' being able to run away with this one.

"We needed some of those runs we had," said Coach Flannery. "Our depth was instrumental."

St. Ignatius did take away the St. Ed's game of pounding the ball inside on offense. As a result, the Eagles took more jump shots than usual. Walters hit three threes. Nichols and Will Meyer assisted on two of them. Vuyancih hit a key jumper from the corner at the buzzer to end the first half in favor of St. Ed's, 28-16.

"With this team it is no one man; everybody could score," Walters said after the game. "We just look for the open man. Everyone scores; we are well-rounded. They're our No. 1 rivals and it was my last time playing them at home. We're going to remember it the rest of our lives."

By the end of the game, it was a rout, the Eagles moving to 9-1 with a 61-34 win.

The next game would be a real test, again one set up by a national schedule.

Much like the prior year when the Eagles were to play Mater Dei on Martin Luther King Day, they would get another jewel of an opponent in Hargrave Military Academy on the Monday holiday. In 2013 on MLK Day, Mater Dei had come in as one of the top-five ranked teams in the country and the No. 1 team in California.

The student section was loaded and played a big factor in the Eagles' upsetting Mater Dei and gaining more national recognition. Certainly, the fans would be out for this one against Hargrave, the student section in full costume garb. The game was sold out and fans who tried to walk up and buy tickets prior to the start of the game were turned down.

This student fan section would carry on throughout the playoffs and to the state championship game. While the home games always attracted fans, the road games didn't always have the following they had had in recent years. In years past, the Eagles could be in a regional in Toledo (at least one and a half hours away) and only have a few hundred fans attending.

"It was frustrating," Coach Flannery commented in recalling those days. "Part of us understood that playing a Wednesday in Toledo or even a weekend in Toledo meant a two-hour ride. There wasn't a whole lot of support from the administration that way. That really changed when Jim Kubacki (current president and former principal) and Gene Boyer (former principal), toward the end of his tenure, made a conscious effort to get somebody at the school outside of the coaching staff to build that unity and pride."

"The last couple years we have had a good group of administrators who have made that a focus and a mission to provide one or two buses to playoff games," Coach Flannery said.

When people go to St. Edward games now there is fan support and there is student support, a presence that has grown within the last seven years.

"Early on in my tenure the fan support was low," Coach Flannery said. "It's made a comeback and is now in the highest it's ever been in the history of the school."

For home games, road games or playoff games, it is not as easy for student fans to travel to the games as it may be at most other schools.

"We're not a small community," Coach Flannery said. "We're not like some schools, where everyone lives five minutes away and can go to the game Friday night and go home – walk to school and walk to the gym. These students are in the classroom first and then they are in another sport or extracurricular – they are all involved in something. To either stick around school here until 7:30 or 8 at night or to go home and come back, often taking as much as 45 minutes in travel time, to support a team is something.

"People might say there is a bad crowd one night. We have students who have three hours of homework on a Tuesday night. It's unrealistic for a place like this to expect kids to show up and be at every game. I have heard this from teachers, administrators, and other coaches that the guys on this team were well liked and well supported by their classmates. The guys on this team supported other teams just as much. If someone went to a football game, he would see the basketball team crowded together somewhere in the middle of the student section. When one shows that support for other people, they get it back."

For Hargrave, the fans came out in full support.

With the fan support already an asset, the other two ingredients needed to pull off an upset was preparation and adaptation.

"As coaches, when we prepare our team going in, we want to play a certain way, but we also coach so that we are ready," Coach Flannery said. "When we practice, we practice everything. We practice to play fast; we practice to play slow. We practice to play against zone defenses and man defenses. We don't always know if they could play really fast or really slow. This team in practice showed us that they could do both. We could execute the half court, but we also had the athleticism to get up and down the floor."

The team's depth would play a factor against Hargrave.

"When teams were playing us fast, we were playing them really well," Coach Flannery said. "I think that some teams try to slow us down. It might have made the game a little closer, but our guys played well and adapted to that. We have different lineups that we could go to. Our depth was a big reason we were successful playing different styles."

A lot of teams didn't have that luxury of bringing off the bench a 6-foot-9-inch student-athlete such as Funderburk, who is a potential high-major player. They could also bring in Parente off the bench to play against the zone because he is a shooter. He could stretch out the zone and make some shots.

"With the point guard, Malcolm Walters can go up and down as well as anybody. Pat Riley could play the half court as well as anybody," Coach Flannery said.

The depth of the team had also generated the interest of the student fans who dubbed them the "Bench Mob."

Hargrave is a school for boys in grades 7-12 with an extra year of post graduate study. Out of Chatham, Virginia, Hargrave actually has a varsity team and a prep team. The varsity team is primarily made up of juniors and seniors and some sophomores. The prep ("PG" or Post Graduate) team is composed of mostly 13th graders. This meant that the Eagles would be playing a team of boys/men older than they, some of them 19 or 20. There was one senior on the team and the rest were post graduates.

In addition to being older, Hargrave had about four student-athletes on the prep team in the 6-foot-8 to 7-foot range. So for the first time this season the Eagles would not have the height advantage against the opponent. On top of that, Hargrave had several Division I recruits. Thus, that adapting to different styles and different match ups would come into play.

Members of the Hargrave team hailed from seven different states.

Coupled with the win against St. Ignatius two nights earlier, the 83-67, victory against Hargrave Military Academy gave the Eagles an outstanding weekend. The Eagles (10-1, ranked No. 1 in Ohio and No. 15 in the nation at the time) never trailed and led by as many as 20 points.

The win brought even more national attention to a program that continues to have presence on the entire USA map more and more each year.

"Our home crowd has a lot to do with it," Coach Flannery said. "You talk about an intimidation factor; teams who come in here have no idea what they are getting themselves into."

As was becoming a trademark for this St. Edward team, the Eagles went on an early 15-0 run in the first quarter with Nichols scoring 13 of those points.

"They tie their shoes the same way as we do," said Nichols, who scored a game-high 29 points. "We came to play basketball. We came with swagger and confidence."

The 29 points was a season high for Nichols. "It's all about the win," Nichols said. "As long as the team wins, I am OK with any number of points I score."

Funderburk came off the bench to have an impressive third quarter when the Tigers were threatening, including pulling to within five points at one juncture. He scored 12 of his career-high 18 points in the third quarter. Hamilton finished with 20 points.

"I turned to some of the coaches at the end of the game and said, 'Wow,' because it was not something we expected to do," Coach Flannery said. "We expected to keep it close and maybe have a shot at the lead and maybe win with a late shot."

What emerged in this game was St. Edward's ability to destroy a defensive press and to play any style of game.

"I remember that Hargrave game I came to," said Brian Ansberry, the former St. Ed's assistant coach. "They full-court pressed the heck out of us and swoosh we went right through them. I don't think any team could press this team successfully. They could play any style and close it down."

With all these big wins under their belts, the Eagles had to guard against complacency and avoid peaking at the wrong time.

While St. Ed's is a program that avoids overdoing it, it does not mean that the Eagles are not a well-conditioned team or that they are afraid to play three games in three days. After all, they played four games in four days while in California.

This conditioning helped the Eagles jump out to huge leads and subsequently they wore down their opponents in 2013-14. This team beat teams and beat good teams fairly easily by wide scores.

A sub coming into the game for the coaches had better do his job. His job was to keep the lead.

"Even the guys who came in maybe knew they had to keep the lead because there are guys behind them prompting the, 'I need to play hard and I need to play well otherwise I'm coming out,'" Coach Flannery said. "With one minute to go in the first quarter, we're not resting. We're putting in other guys who are busting their butts and playing hard. Midway through the second quarter, some teams are breathing heavy and it's getting to halftime and we are still coming at them and putting the pressure on them. We can do things with fresh legs and guys who want to play hard. If we are winning by 10 at halftime, the first four minutes (of the third quarter) are very important. This (the lead) has to be 15, not five after about three or four minutes (of the second half)."

They were to need such gas in the last weekend of January when the Eagles had three games scheduled in three days – Friday against Cleveland Heights, Saturday against Benedictine, and Sunday against Huntington Prep of West Virginia.

Against Cleveland Heights on the road, the Eagles found themselves down early. Instead of rushing off to a big lead, the Eagles found themselves on the back end of such a run. The Tigers smelled upset as they opened a 15-4 lead. The Eagles then went on an 8-0 spurt to cut it to 15-12 and started using their depth in the second quarter to mount a 35-26 halftime lead.

The Eagles really turned on the jets in the third quarter to take a commanding 68-36 lead on the way to moving to 11-1 and maintaining their No. 1 ranking in the state with an 84-54 win. Nichols had 25 points to lead all scorers. Vuyancih had two threes and wound up with 14 points. Hamilton also had 14 points.

If the win against Cleveland Heights was a rout, the next night's win against Benedictine was even more lopsided, with the Eagles walking away with a 96-52 win. Sixteen different players scored for the Eagles that night.

Like Heights, Benedictine kept it close early but a late first-quarter flurry gave the Eagles a 21-11 lead after one quarter. The Eagles were moving the ball around in the first quarter, with Walters assisting Nichols, Nichols assisting Ryan on a dunk, Walters assisting Hamilton, and Hamilton assisting Vuyancih.

The second-team crew was on the floor before the first period was completed. Much of that continued into the second period as Meyer came off the bench to score eight points in the second period – all on put-backs. He wound up with 10 points for the night – all on put-backs.

"That's usually what I do," Meyer said. "That's how I get my points. I get down low, get the rebound and put it back up."

The Eagles were supposed to play Huntington Prep in Chas Wolfe's Dunk-4-Diabetes Showcase at Walsh University in North Canton. Another school with 13th graders and a school that has sent numerous players on to collegiate careers, Huntington Prep must have learned about the Hargrave game. Prep backed out of the game. Allegedly it did not want to play two games in two days. In California, St. Edward played two games in one day. On this weekend the Eagles were playing three games in three days.

Since Huntington Prep was to be the Eagles' last out-of-state opponent, the Eagles could lay claim to beating at least one team from five different states. Instead of Huntington Prep, the Eagles would play Walnut Hills from Cincinnati.

As it was against Cleveland Heights, the Eagles fell behind in this one, trailing by as many as 10 points in the second quarter. Eventually, the Eagles moved on to 13-1 with a 64-53 victory.

Senior Marsalis "Sal" Hamilton was named the MVP of the game for his 15 points, four assists, six rebounds, three steals and one blocked shot. It was the second time Sal Hamilton was named the MVP of a showcase during this season.

"In the first half we were just taking the time to get a feel for what they do," said Hamilton. "In the second half, we made them speed it up, making them take shots they didn't want to take."

Funderburk came off the bench to block two shots with the ball practically landing in the next county each time.

"He is like a safety net back there," Hamilton said. "If one of us gets beat off the dribble, he's right back there to clean it up."

"Vuyancih did a great job on their player in the second half," Coach Flannery said.

Nichols put up some nice numbers offensively. He was 10-of-14 at the free-throw line, grabbed eight rebounds and had a team-high 20 points. Vuyancih finished with 11 points with a perfect 3-of-3 at the line. Ryan had nine points and five rebounds. He made 3-of-4 charity tosses. Funderburk had seven rebounds and seven points to go with his two blocked shots and a steal.

The Eagles' winning streak was now at nine games.

Chapter 8

Worthiness in Offseason Preparation

Basketball, such as most other student-athletic activities, has become a year-round sport. The participation of student-athletes in summer leagues has morphed into full-length AAU games and tournaments, shootouts and showcases during the offseason.

While Coach Flannery has been a big part of USA Basketball in Colorado over the past 13 summers, he does not necessarily believe in one concentrating on basketball 24/7.

"I don't believe a whole lot in this off-season activity; I think we overdo it today," Coach Flannery said. "I heard something about how parents need to support their children in what they do but not necessarily direct and guide them as they do so much today. So much of today is forcing them and making sure they are working out and going to the gym and putting up shots."

This in turn means that coaches feel the pressure to be constantly doing something for their student-athletes, because everyone else is doing it.

"I'm a big believer in getting away," Coach Flannery said. "These players don't want to hear me year round. If they do, they start to tune me out. These student-athletes need to have a life because they are teenagers. Go have fun. Go play baseball. Go do something else. Yes, I like basketball-only guys because they become more talented in basketball when they are focused on basketball, but I don't hold it against guys who play other sports. I played other sports when I was a student-athlete. I would be a hypocrite to say one can't play other sports."

When talking about the off season, so many schools play in summer leagues. They are getting their student-athletes for five or 10 nights and they are playing games.

"A couple years ago I just said enough is enough and I stopped doing it," Coach Flannery said. "We had to separate our teams and we couldn't play them all. I am not going to establish my starting lineup in the summer when these players are competing for spots later. We cut back. The shootouts are just a weekend when we could bring our guys together and we get to see some competition. There is some good."

The Eagles get together two times a week during the off season.

"Most people might think that it is not enough and to me that is crazy, because it is way more than we ever did when I was a kid," Coach Flannery said. "People's mentality today is that they have to keep going, but these players can get hurt and lose their focus. That hurts my team in the long run."

On the other hand, offseason activities have helped the Eagles to bond, and they have also given them a gauge as to how good they could be the next season. "I thought we could win the state championship as early as last summer from how we looked in one of these shootouts in Massillon and Canton," said Tom Bodle, a St. Ed's assistant coach and director of basketball operations. "Some of the better teams were down there – Uniontown Lake and Moeller (No. 1 in state at the end of year in AP poll in '13 and '14). We played them even, without Marsalis, who was out with an injury. Kipper played sparingly because he was out with an injury. We lost to Uniontown by a point."

The depth of the 2014 championship team took its form in the off season even though the Eagles didn't overdo it. Ansberry recalls a similar experience when he was on the 1998 state championship team.

"We would go to summer leagues early in Flan's career," Coach Ansberry said. "Then we would go to summer shootouts for a week. We once went to the Wheeling Jesuit University Shootout, which we won. There were teams from West Virginia and Ohio. We bonded then too.

During the year we went down and played Wheeling Park. Bonding, traveling and having success against out-of-state teams are the huge things about becoming a team."

That was in the 1990s. Since then, Coach Flannery's philosophy on off-season activities has changed to avoid overdoing it.

"My philosophy in the off season is to get away, relax, and work on one's game," Coach Flannery said. "It is true; players are made in the off season, but they need to work on their own to develop their skills and to get bigger and stronger. I am no longer going to be in their faces and make them do it."

As well as a student-athlete learns, a coach also learns with time.

"Coaches have big egos, as do I," Coach Flannery said. "We think we need to be in control of everything. The greatest thing I have learned as a coach is to let go and not take myself so seriously."

In Ohio all basketball teams are prohibited to practice for 30 days after the season ends and all of August.

"I use that rule to the T," Coach Flannery said. "Some people might say that I have talent so it doesn't really matter. How I control that talent and how to use it and implement it and motivate it is the bigger picture. There are times I just need to get away from the scene. I need to reenergize myself. I need to have the players reenergize themselves. Some come back after summer and they are more tired than when they left. People are pushing them in different directions. They are working so hard that it becomes counterproductive."

Former St. Ed's and Michigan State standout Delvon Roe is the perfect example. He'll admit it to this day. Back when he was a junior, he was the first player Flannery had who was invited to the USA Basketball tryouts/trials with him.

"When I brought him out there I had discussions with Delvon and his dad, who also admits to it," Coach Flannery reflected. "I always told them they are doing too much and working too hard. His dad was crazy. He would make him lift weights and run and swim and then go to the gym. When I say they would work out two, three, four hours a day, I am not exaggerating. They would do it every single day – work, work. I noticed Delvon, the kid. I could see him breaking down physically."

Roe was an elite player. He had a chance to go wherever he wanted for college. When he was at USA with the group, he hurt his shoulder. He was the leading scorer and one of the leading rebounders in the entire camp, which featured the 30 best players in the country.

"We could tell he was getting tired," Coach Flannery said. "I had the conversation with him. I said, 'Delvon, you have to take off the next month.' I said, 'You have to take the whole month of July and some of August and lie on your couch and be a kid. Stop working out and take 30 days off and just get your body healed. Let everything kind of catch up.' He said, 'Coach, I can't. I am just not programmed that way. I need to work and I need to work hard.' 'I understand it,' I told him, 'but I am just trying to give you some advice.' He kept working. He didn't really listen."

At the start of his senior year he would need micro fracture surgery and missed nearly the entire season because of deterioration of his knees. It was due to too much work. He had basically worked himself into the ground.

"When we were growing up, we'd go hang out in the neighborhood and fool around and play," Coach Flannery said. "These guys don't do that any more. These guys go to the gym, they go to the weight room, and they play AAU."

Delvon Blanton, Roe's dad and an assistant coach on the 2014 championship team, wishes he and his son would have listened.

"That's something coach Flan and I talk about to this day," Coach Blanton said. "He (Flannery) knows that I am aggressive in the gym. I like to work kids out and push their buttons. Coach Flan told me at the time and I just didn't listen because I didn't see it coming. I was looking for so much success in my son that and I never considered at the time that it could occur. He was so right about what he told my son, but I had never been in that situation so I didn't know. When I look back upon it, my son and I talk about it to this day and realize what Coach Flan said. We overdid it and overworked and what happened is that his body broke down."

Today Coach Blanton tells the players a different story.

"We're going to go for an hour," Coach Blanton said. "That's all you get, I tell them. I am not going to overwork your body. I am not going to break your body down because you are too young. To be in the gym for three hours every day, you don't need that. He (Coach Flan) always teaches and is always on us about giving days off. Don't overwork them and I listen to him now. Coach Flan doesn't want you guys to be in here seven days a week. He wants you to get two days of rest, come back Monday and go hard.

"Delvon's body broke down from too much traveling, running from tournament to tournament and camp to camp. He came back to AAU and to high school. He did that for three years straight. He never got a break. I never saw it coming because I didn't look for it. He wasn't telling me anything until his senior year when he said, 'Dad, my legs hurt.' It just didn't register. He said he had a little pain, but I never looked at it like he had an injury. We took him to the hospital and it was as Flan had said, overwork. He never recovered. I look back on what Flan said in those five years and I tell kids now like Kipper and D.J., who will do a lot of traveling with AAU, to take a good three weeks off in August and rest. Now the guys listen and learn. I've learned from that."

Coach Flannery, in avoiding overdoing it, does enough with his team, but avoids making the game more about the coaches than about the student-athletes.

"I'm a parent and I have the same schedule," Coach Flannery said. "My week is booked with my children's activities. Back when we were growing up, we came home from school and went outside, came home to do our homework and went to bed. We might play in a recreation league on the weekend. Now kids are practicing during the week all year round. They are practicing basketball one night, baseball the next night, another extracurricular the next night. It's insane, but our society has created this situation. As a parent, I feel I have to do the same thing."

Flannery also realizes that the olden days will never return.

"We're caught in a tough spot," he said. "There is a lot of good in keeping busy, and I am not even saying that I am right about moderating one's activities. Someone else might see this and say, 'Coach, that's the dumbest thing I've ever heard.' I'm OK with that. We move too fast. Coaches do a lot of things just to make themselves feel better. Even when we run practice, we put in all these drills and we make them fancy. In reality, it doesn't do anything for our players or our teams. We might practice for three hours and say we had a three-hour practice today, but the student-athletes were disinterested and didn't get much out of it. I think that is life in general any more. We are scheduling and doing so much that we are overdoing everything and the players are tuning out."

Most people are busy during the day. Some of it good and some of it bad and the parents are getting involved in a huge manner.

"When I was a young kid, our parents didn't even come to the games," Coach Flannery said. "Our lives are so structured compared to when we were growing up. A lot of that has to do with the parents' lives. Both parents are working, or we have parents who are separated. If a youth wants to play basketball, he has to play in a league game or on a travel team if he wants that kind of competition. At least that is our perception. As parents, we have to schedule our children's lives around what we are doing. When we were growing up, I had Mom at home and all the kids just ran around and did what they wanted to do. There is definitely some social benefit to that. Today it is that necessary evil that things have to be structured and organized. I don't want to be a hypocrite as a parent. I tell my children to go out and play all the time. When they have no one to play with because no one else is doing the same, it is hard to do. This is the society we live in."

This need to get ahead at all costs leads to more individualism and less teamwork, which hurts a group of student-athletes in a team sport like basketball.

"In today's day and age, it is hard getting them to buy into being a good teammate," Coach Flannery said. "They get into the AAU mentality. If they don't like their coach or they don't like their team, they leave. They find another team. If they lose a game at 8 o'clock in the morning, they play another game at noon so they really don't care. It's, 'I just lost, but it is no big deal. I am going to go play another game.' If they don't compete or they don't win the tournament, well, they have another tournament next weekend so they are OK. That's what the AAU mentality is. Some people say it is bad coaching, but that is not the case in most situations. AAU's problem is lack of loyalty and competitiveness."

This carries on to the regular season for high school basketball and can tear a team apart and hamper its chances of attaining its goals.

"The way it is affecting high school basketball is that we as coaches deal with a mentality of 'if I am not playing, I am going to go somewhere else,' or, 'I don't really care if we win or lose; I just want my son to play.' It's hurting our sport. The longer I have been here as a coach the more I have witnessed the 'I don't care' thinking."

As well as in AAU around town, some players at other high schools have moved around from school to school as if they were free agents. This merely emphasizes the individuality and the "getting that college scholarship at all costs" mentality. It makes it hard for a student-athlete to convince someone that he is worthy of his jersey.

Chapter 9

Last Play History, Next Play Now

Perhaps the one element that kept the Eagles focused on winning the state championship game was the "next-play" concept. By "next play" it is meant that one cannot do anything about what just happened, good or bad. It goes back to the mind candy – the present is a gift. The final seconds of the game are a gift because the Eagles have kept that next-play focus, constantly homed in on what to do next rather than worrying about five steps ahead or dwelling on four or five steps behind.

"We have to coach that way," said Tom Bodle, an assistant coach and the director of basketball operations. "If we focus on something we just did, good or bad, that was that moment and now we have a new moment. That other team, the official, or the crowd doesn't care what we did a moment ago or the game before. They are ready to make their play, and we have to be ready to make our play.

"There is forgiveness when student-athletes make mistakes. If he has a bad day and sits out, the next day is a new practice. We tell them, 'Keep your head straight, work hard, and get your spot back.' That's the way we have to coach to be successful. Otherwise we are going to get kids brooding, coaches upset. I've watched Flan coach for nearly 20 years and it has been very effective. The players who don't want to go by that give up. The school is stronger and the team is stronger because of that. The good kids are going to stick with that and improve and say, 'Hey one shot isn't going to kill me.'"

Without a next-play mentality, a mole hill of mistakes can turn into a mountain of one and then there will be no escape.

"We keep reminding these guys of a saying that I got from Mike Krzyzewski --- it is *next play*," Coach Flannery said. "Next play is the mentality that someone has to have in sport. Move on to the next play or one mistake will become two mistakes. As a player, I might turn the ball over when I am playing and if I sulk or pout about it, I am going to make another mistake. I am going to let my team down. We pound that into their heads during practice – the next play, the next play. The coaches say, 'You made a mistake. Everyone makes a mistake. You better get back and play defense. You better play smart from here on forward.' The same thing applies to games – next play, next game. Let's move on. We did our job, enjoy it tonight. Feel good about it for the time being and let's get back to work and focus on what we need to do to get better to keep winning. That's the kind of philosophy we use – big picture."

The next-play concept was carried into the eventual state championship game. There next-play focus translated into high efficiency.

"We did what we were good at very well," Coach Nugent said. "We kept getting better as the year went on at what we were about. Any time we had a hiccup, we got back to who we were. We always return to what we do well, being a good defensive team, being a team that looks to push out and get into transition and get to the rim as much as we can, and hitting shots."

What made the team so efficient was that that next play would often come from the bench. This gave fans who watched this team the treat of knowing that what came after the starters hardly lacked any luster.

Not only was this next-play attitude evident in a game, but it was seen throughout the season. Such was the case in the 2001-2002 campaign.

After the three games in three days swing during the 2013-14 season, the St. Ed's team would keep its winning streak alive by trouncing state-ranked Gilmour and St. John's Jesuit on the same weekend.

The victory over Toledo St. John's was a huge one. Any time a win against St. John's is remarkable, and it doesn't happen very often. St. John's could serve as a gauge as to how good a St. Edward team might be. Additionally, the St. John's encounters could serve as learning experiences. Such was the case during the 2001-2002 season, when evidence of the next-play concept carried from the mid season to the post season.

The 2001-2002 St. Ed's basketball team had had the "next play" in mind between the two times it had played St. John's that year as it did not worry about the recent past and focused only on what was immediately ahead.

The second St. John's game came during an astounding run. This was one of the lesser talented teams at St. Ed's during Flannery's tenure, yet it eventually made it to the final four. They could have won a state championship. Only a couple points and couple minutes had prevented the Eagles from advancing to the championship game.

That year they played St. John's in Toledo during the season and the Titans were ranked No. 1 in the state at the time. St. Ed's lost by 28 points. Simply put, they were blown out of the gym. It was one of their few losses that year.

"After that game we talked about a lot of things that we could do better to compete at that level," Coach Flannery recalled. "When we think of a 30-point loss, we could think, man, we are nowhere near as good as that team. We have to take into consideration that it was at their place. The refs might have helped them out. It was the way we played -- we played terribly, timidly. We missed easy shots and some free throws. We lacked effort. We talked about those things and watched film of it. I just simply showed them this was the effort that needed to be there. These were the positions we needed to be in on defense in order to get stops. We need to make layups and get free throws. Everyone should be able to do that (thinking of the next play)."

After a big victory against St. Ignatius in Gund Arena, the Eagles would have a chance to play the Titans in the regional finals at the University of Toledo. The Titans were 25-0 at the time and ranked No. 1 in the state. Leading up to that game, the coaching staff watched the film of that game again. They went through every possession, noting how they scored and what they did better and what St. Ed's didn't do and how the Eagles could have done better. Then Coach Flannery eliminated a few things.

"If we made a few layups, now it's a 20-point game," Coach Flannery explained. "If we eliminate a couple of bad calls during the game, maybe it's a 10-point game. Now take away some of our mental mistakes and lack of effort in certain areas and we could beat this team."

Sure enough, Neil Fronhapple hit a shot at the buzzer and the Eagles knocked out the No. 1 team in the state in the regional finals in Toledo to go to the final four. The impact of the learning experience from the first game against St. John's and the second one was immeasurable.

"That's what we use when we lose; there is a reason why we lose," Coach Flannery explained. "Sometimes it is just talent. Sometimes teams are just better than we are and we have to live with that. A lot of times we can find little things to make our team better. Sometimes players don't listen as much when we win. They just say, 'Hey, what we are doing is working – we are winning and we don't need to do anything better.'

"After a loss, for one thing, I have their attention. They know they need to get better, because someone out there is better than they are. They need to start listening. We watch some film and start breaking some things down, identifying what each individual player needs to do to get better. For all our teams, those first two or three losses are great teaching moments. We have to learn, and we have to try to get better (thinking next play). I'm blessed here at St. Ed's that we have enough talent to compete even if we are outmatched (such as against St. John's in 2002)."

If they can compete and keep games close, they can find ways to beat teams, with the next-play thinking in place. That's the approach that Coach Flannery takes and is one of the reasons why they have had success in the tournaments. They have that confidence that they can beat anybody no matter what their record was during the year. A lot of times when they've had such losses, it is because their schedule was so tough.

Going along with the next-play mentality are the lessons to be learned from a loss.

Another example of how the Eagles learned this lesson from a loss and used it to form the mindset that they could beat anyone came in the '98 season, the other state championship year. They were in the Slam Dunk to the Beach Tournament, a national tournament in Delaware. They had lost to Dunbar from Baltimore. St. Ed's had a good basketball team, and this was its first loss. The Eagles had won their first few games that year and were nationally ranked in the top 10 in the country at the time.

"It might not have been an upset because they were very good, but we didn't play very well," Coach Flannery said. "Even back then, what I tell my teams is that this one is on me. Steve Lepore stopped me and said, 'Coach, this is on us. We need to get better. We need to focus. We need to play harder.' We lost the game, but it brought out that emotion and some of that leadership. I knew at that point that these players, like the 2013-14 group, took ownership of that team. Steve Lepore was the guy that spoke up, similar to Tony Vuyancih on the 2014 team. It's moments like that – it sometimes takes a loss to bring it out of them."

The loss to Dunbar turned out to be the only loss for the '98 team. By thinking next play, they won the rest of their games, posting a 26-1 season and a state championship.

As will be learned in Chapter 11, the idea of learning from a loss and learning in general will enable a team to stay focused on the next play and ultimately be worthy of the jersey.

Chapter 10

Losing With Dignity a Worthy Act

With the three-games-in three-days weekend behind them, the Eagles returned home to play against Gilmour Academy, a Brothers of Holy Cross school in Gates Mills, Ohio, that is a sister school to St. Ed's. Although a smaller school than St. Ed's, Gilmour was a formidable opponent. Entering the game, the 12-1 Lancers were ranked fifth in the state in Division III.

Gilmour came into the game with a 12-game winning streak while the Eagles were riding a nine-game winning streak.

For the third time in the last four games, the Eagles would not go on an early run and take a big lead, but rather they found themselves behind in the first quarter.

The Eagles were down by as many as eight points in the first quarter, 11-3, and had to hustle to regain the lead, keep it, and build upon it. They did so in the first, second and third periods, respectively.

"It's not going to be the same night in and night out," Coach Flannery said. "I don't think it is anything we are doing differently."

After falling behind early, the Eagles went on a 12-0 run to take a 15-11 lead in the first quarter. Nichols, who finished with a game-high 28 points, hit a three, Marsalis "Sal" Hamilton scored off a steal, Nichols scored again by taking it to the basket hard, Hamilton scored on a three with an assist from Nichols and Meyer scored on his trademark put-back.

The Lancers were able to recapture the lead in the second quarter after tying the game, 15-15, at the end of the first. Flannery was platoon substituting in the first and second quarters. Funderburk came off the bench to score on a put-back to make it 20-19 with 5:46 to go in the half. The basket resulted in the Eagles going up for good.

"We had a hard time scoring and we had a hard time stopping them," Coach Flannery said.

Andrew Dowell assisted Nichols at 4:07 of the third period to make it 52-42. Then the Eagles went on a 19-2 run to take a 71-46 lead by the midway point of the fourth quarter.

Five different Eagles – Nichols, Hamilton, Malcolm Walters, Flannery and Connor Pisco – hit threes on the evening. Hamilton finished with 22 points. Funderburk scored 12 off the bench. The Eagles won, 83-57, to move to 14-1 and extend their winning streak to 10 games.

Always a test for St. Edward is a game against St. John's, perennially one of the top ranked big-school teams in the state.

St. John's had won 14 of its previous 15 games and was highly ranked in the state.

Playing with a short lead for most of the night, St. Edward's basketball team avoided trailing on the way to a 66-59 win, in Toledo.

"It's been a while since we have beaten St. John's," said Coach Flannery after the game. "This is a tough place to play."

The Eagles' biggest lead had been only 12 points and that came late in the game. For most of the night they led by an average of five or seven points.

Nichols scored a career-high 31 points while logging a lot of minutes with very few breathers.

"I want to do whatever is asked of me," said Nichols, who was signing autographs for fans after the game. "If it means extra minutes, guarding a certain player, getting free throws, getting rebounds, or scoring a few extra points, I'll do it to make this team the best."

On the other end was defense. For the second time in the last three games, Vuyancih was asked to guard the top scorer on the other team. This time it was A.J. Glover, Jr.

"I like when the coaches ask me to be on the top scorer of the other team," said Vuyancih. "I like to draw my energy from playing defense.

A lot of people might not like defense. I get a lot of energy from locking up the other guy."

St. Ed's did jump out to a 9-0 lead and it had the makings of another rout, but this was in St. John's domain with a roaring student section behind one of the baskets. The Eagles led by as many as 11 points early in the first quarter, but St. John's was able to cut it to two points four different times and to one point once in the second quarter.

Meyer had another good game off the bench.

"Will Meyer is the glue that not many people know about," Coach Flannery said. "He might not be the glory MVP, but he is the MVP of a lot of little things that don't show up in the stats. He never lets the team down."

Riley assisted Nichols and Nichols assisted Meyers on threes midway through the third quarter as the Eagles maintained a 5-to-7 point edge.

After the win against St. John's, the Eagles would travel to St. Ignatius and use their bread-and-butter – good defense – to pull out a win.

A team's staging comebacks during the course of a season, such as the one in 2002 with St. John's, starts with mini comebacks within games. When the Eagles are behind and need to claw back, they think about the next play. In many cases, this is done with defensive stops that are then converted into transition baskets that eventually translate into wins.

"My M.O. here has been to be a defensive-oriented coach," Coach Flannery said. "At this level, we have to play great defense. That keeps us in games. The better defensive team we are, the better we are going to be. Every night we can control how we are defensively with effort and just being in the right spot. Good teams will make shots, but we should always have a good defensive night.

"There are nights we are not going to shoot the ball well, resulting in a bad offensive night. There is no excuse not to have a good defensive night. The 2014 team wanted to win with good defense. We hung our hats on our half-court man-to-man. At some point somewhere along the line, we are going to have to get a stop to win a game."

The defensive-minded approach coupled with the next-play thinking came to be huge factors against St. Ignatius. Coming into the St. Ignatius game, the Eagles had won 11 straight games, but knew that it is always tough to win in Sullivan Gymnasium in the Ohio City neighborhood of

Cleveland. In the first meeting between the two teams, St. Ignatius had a defensive strategy of its own, which was to push the Eagles to the outside and deny them from pounding the ball inside. With its home crowd as an asset, the Wildcats again tried to take the Eagles out of their game. The Wildcats would not only use some defensive strategy but would also show comeback capability of their own.

The Eagles led most of the first three quarters until the Cats tied it at the end of the third quarter, 45-45. The third-quarter flurry stretched into the fourth quarter as the Wildcats went on a 15-2 run to take an eight-point lead, 53-45, with six minutes to go in regulation. It appeared as if Ignatius might be getting its home win and that St. Ed's might suffer its first loss of the season to an Ohio team.

Captains are supposed to come through in the toughest times. Marsalis "Sal" Hamilton scored all nine of St. Edward's points in the final 3:24 of regulation as the Eagles were able to get the needed defensive stops. In turn they were able to get the offensive opportunities to stop the Wildcats. They learned from the mind candy that "if it is important to you, you will find a way and if it is not, you will find an excuse." They also remembered what Coach Flannery had said about there being no excuses for a bad defensive night.

In addition to putting it on his shoulders late in the game, Hamilton would ignite things in overtime, scoring the first St. Ed's basket. "That's what clutch players do," Coach Flannery said. "We are lucky to have two clutch players like that – Marsalis and Kipper Nichols. We want the ball in their hands when it matters. Kipper came up big with a three pointer." Down 64-63, Nichols canned a three-point shot from the right wing with 2:08 left to give the Eagles a two-point lead. Ignatius was never to see the lead again that night.

The Wildcats did tie the game, 66-66, but Ryan also came up clutch on this night. With 49 seconds to play, Walters flipped a pass inside to Ryan who worked his way inside and put the ball up. The ball rolled around and went in, and Ryan was fouled. He converted on the old-fashioned three-point play to make it 72-68.

"Malcolm's one of the best players on the team," Ryan said. "In that situation, he looked at me and he looked at the basket. Once he got the ball to me, I knew I was going to score. The Ignatius fans were really hyped and I just had to think through it and make the free throw."

With the Eagles up, 73-70, St. Ignatius tried a three-point shot at the buzzer, but it didn't make the mark and the Eagles dodged a bullet in winning their 12th straight. To go 2-0 against St. Ignatius during the regular season is quite an accomplishment for an Eagle team. To do it after being down eight points in the fourth quarter and having to go through overtime in Ohio City demonstrated what this team might be made of. It reinforced the idea that it could be a state championship team. Next-play thinking also played a role. The experience would prove vital three days removed from the win and again in the state championship game.

"We had some experiences during the year when we needed that next-play mentality," Coach Flannery said. "We talked about this throughout the year, but it doesn't always translate into success. The players might not pick it up wholeheartedly, but these guys bought into it. They only worried about, 'What could I do now just to play well?'"

While the Eagles showed that they could come back in the second St. Ignatius game, another big test would come the following Tuesday at Shaker Heights when it was to be, according to the local Cleveland media, No. 1 St. Edward against No. 2 (in the Greater Cleveland area) Shaker Heights. Over the years, St. Ed's and Shaker Heights had had many great battles in basketball, going all the way back to the late Bob Wonson days at Shaker.

Before the game was even played, the Eagles received a big blow when D.J. Funderburk turned his foot in practice on Monday, breaking it. All indications were that he would be out for the season. For a team that relies a lot on its bench, this was a real setback for the second five, who had been called on so many times during the season to help wear down the opponents.

Funderburk was missed as the Eagles had a late rally, demonstrating the same type of comeback capability and next-play mentality they had against Ignatius, but nevertheless they fell, 53-50.

The Eagles, who dropped to 16-2 with the first and only loss to an Ohio team, were in the game early and late; but in between those two segments, they had a very off night. They shot 26 percent from the field on 15-of-58.

"It wasn't that we didn't play well enough at the end to come back and win," Coach Eric Flannery said after the game. "It's that we just did not play well for about 30 minutes of the game. Shaker Heights did play well."

"We played poorly throughout the game," Coach Flannery said. "After the first five minutes we became very tentative. We were selfish. We took really bad shots and stopped attacking the rim again, which is what we had done against Ignatius. We did not execute offensively and did not play particularly good defense."

Shaker threw a zone at St. Ed's that prevented the Eagles from executing as they normally do. Despite that, the Eagle again never gave up until the final buzzer and nearly pulled it out in the end.

The Eagles were down, 50-39, with a minute and a half to go, but did not quit. Nichols hit a pair of free throws to make it 50-41. Sal Hamilton's basket made it 51-43. Vuyancih hit a three with an assist from Walters to make it 52-46. After a defensive stop, Nichols scored on a put-back with 31 seconds to go to make it 52-48. Hamilton then stole the ball in the backcourt and scored on a layup to make it a two-point game, 52-50, with 29 seconds to go.

Darien Knowles then stole the ball and the Eagles had the ball with a chance to tie it or win it as the clock was ticking down; however, they could not get off a decent shot. They had one more chance to shoot the three as the buzzer sounded but could not bury it.

When they lost to Shaker, they lost the No. 1 ranking in Cleveland to Shaker and the No. 1 ranking in the state. It was upsetting for the group, because they knew they had lost some of the things they had.

There have been only two teams in the history of the school that have won an AP state poll championship, in '98 and '07. Yet despite the loss, the Eagles did not give up on the season, maintaining the next-play and worthy-of-the-jersey thinking.

"It was something we could keep these guys focused on," Coach Flannery said. "They could have been saying, 'We are not playing well; we were playing for that (state poll championship) and lost it.' Derek got hurt. A lot of people counted us out at that point, which was maybe a good thing. It took off some pressure."

"Let me tell you this, from a coaching standpoint, it was great to lose that game. We wanted to get focused for the state tournament. Now we had our guys' attention again. Now they are not as good as they think they are. They are kind of hungry again if it turns the way we think it should. I think they were upset for a little while, but then they focused on what they needed to do to get better. It goes back to the focus and thinking about the next play."

The biggest thing they learned they had to do involved X's and O's. They knew they had to be able to attack the zone. Since many teams up to that point had not used a zone, the Eagles didn't have to prepare a whole lot and didn't have a lot of game experience with it. After that more teams threw zones at them.

Teams have bad nights; teams at times come up with their best games. The home-court advantage comes into play, and injured players prove to be a factor. It is impossible to pinpoint the exact reason(s) for a loss.

They also learned from the Ignatius games that teams were going to try different things defensively to stop the Eagles from scoring.

"It wasn't a direct result (from the first Ignatius game), but we said we had to make some shots and get the other guys involved," Coach Flannery said. "If they wanted to extend the zone, we are going to have to make some shots. Even if we are missing, we have to shoot them. We have to keep everyone honest on the defensive end whether they are playing man or zone. We got better at the guard position because of that."

Learning to lose with grace was also a part of being worthy of the jersey as will be learned in the next chapter.

Coach Eric Flannery with wife Lori (holding son Sean), his father Jim, and mother Judy after the 1998 state championship game.

2014 picture of Coach Eric Flannery's family. (L to R): Sean, Lori, Abigail, Eric, Grace, and P.J. (Photo by Marianne Mangan)

St. Edward "Bench Mob" awaiting the final seconds of the 2014 State Championship game. Jack Flannery, Phil Parente, and Justin Follmer are in the center. (Photo Courtesy of St. Edward HS)

Senior Connor Pisco playing defense against St. Ignatius with Justin Follmer standing behind. (Photo Courtesy of St. Edward HS)

Sean Flannery, Jack Flannery, and Frank Geib in a game versus Firestone. (Photo Courtesy of St. Edward HS)

Senior point guard Malcolm Walters running the show during the state championship game 2014. (Photo Courtesy of St. Edward HS)

Senior captain and emotional leader Tony Vuyancih doing what he does best, defending the opponents' best player. (Photo Courtesy of St. Edward HS)

Senior point guard Pat Riley playing solid defense in the state championship game 2014. (Photo Courtesy of St. Edward HS)

Junior post player Mike Ryan looking to knock down a jump shot during a regular season game in 2014. (Photo Courtesy of St. Edward HS)

Sophomore Derek Funderburk lines up for a free throw during a regular-season game at St. Edward. (Photo Courtesy of St. Edward HS)

Senior utility man Will Meyer is playing defense in the district semifinal game. (Photo Courtesy of St. Edward HS)

Coach Eric Flannery is discussing strategy with senior Phil Parente during game. (Photo Courtesy of St. Edward HS)

Junior Kipper Nichols getting instruction from Coach Eric Flannery. (Photo Courtesy of St. Edward HS)

Delvon Roe '08, after injuring his knee and missing his entire senior season, cheers on his teammates during the 2008 state championship game. (Photo Courtesy of St. Edward HS)

St. Edward 2014 state championship team posing for a photo following the game. (Photo Courtesy of St. Edward HS)

St. Edward 1998 state championship team posing for a photo following game. (Photo Courtesy of St. Edward HS)

USA Basketball staff from (L to R) Trainer David Craig, Eric Flannery, Coach Don Showalter, Coach L.J. Goolsby, and team doctor Herb Parris. (photo courtesy of USA Basketball)

Varsity assistant coaches Steve Logan, Delvon Blanton, Jim Flannery, and Dan Gallagher.

St. Edward JV coaches Josh Nugent and Joe Scarpitti react after a timeout during the 2014 season. (Photo Courtesy of St. Edward HS)

Freshman coaches and father/son duo T.J. and Fran Gallagher discuss strategy during the game. (Photo Courtesy of St. Edward HS)

Junior Varsity assistant coaches for 2014; Jason Bratten, Pete Campbell, and Joe Scarpitti. (Photo Courtesy of St. Edward HS)

Author Norm Weber sitting courtside during the 2014 state championship game. (Photo Courtesy of St. Edward HS)

Freshman coaches Tom Bodle and James Crawford watch their team from the sidelines of a 2014 game. (Photo Courtesy of St. Edward HS)

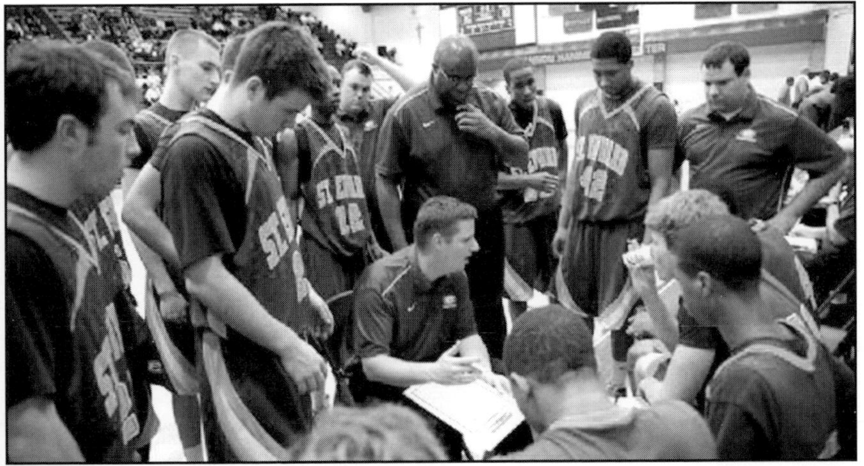

Former assistant coaches Happy Dobbs and Brian Ansberry watch over a huddle during a game in 2010. (Photo Courtesy of St. Edward HS)

Juniors Kipper Nichols and Mike Ryan pose with the state championship trophy after the game. (photo courtesy of St. Edward High School)

Tony Vuyancih surveying the defense in the 2014 state championship game.

The St. Edward student section reacts during the 2014 state championship game in Columbus, OH. (photo courtesy of St. Edward High School)

Members of the 2012 St. Edward Eagles celebrate after winning the regional championship at Cleveland State University. (photo courtesy of St. Edward High School)

Coach Flannery (far right) poses with the River Basketball Association team he played with during his college years. Also pictured are close friends of Flannery: Ryan Spicer (far left), Kevin Neitzel (back middle), Dave McNamee (far right next to Flannery). Also in photo is Mike McLaren, legendary director of the RBA courts (middle front). (photo courtesy of Mike McLaren)

St. Edward vs. Mater Dei, CA in 2013. Mater Dei traveled to St. Edward on MLK day 2013, Mater Dei was ranked #1 in the country. The Eagles won 58-44. (photo courtesy of St. Edward High School)

The St. Edward student section stormed the court after the Eagles upset the #1 team in the country, Mater Dei, in 2013. (photo courtesy of St. Edward High School)

Kipper Nichols and the rest of the team sit on the bench after being upset in the District Championship in 2013. (photo courtesy of St. Edward High School)

Seniors (L to R) Collin Popson, Brandon Simpson, Tim Stainbrook, Royal Eddie, and Zhakir Hillmon hold the district runner-up trophy in 2013. (photo courtesy of St. Edward High School)

Head Coach Eric Flannery with sons Sean and P.J. at his side before accepting the trophy for the 2002 district championship. (Photo Courtesy of St. Edward HS)

Coach Flannery and his sophomore son Sean embrace after the 2014 State. (Photo Courtesy of St. Edward HS)

Coach Eric Flannery addressing the student body in a rally for the 2014 state championship team. (Photo Courtesy of St. Edward HS)

Senior captain Marsalis Hamilton about to receive his medal during the state championship award ceremony. (Photo Courtesy of St. Edward HS)

Coach Flannery and the "Bench Mob" watch on as Marsalis Hamilton releases "The Shot" that sent the 2014 state championship game into overtime. (ImpactActionPhotos.com)

Coach Flannery poses for a picture with Matt and Michael Orbany at a Clips for Cancer event held at St. Edward. Michael was a true inspiration to the entire St. Edward community. #NEGU was Michael's legacy, Never Ever Give Up! (Photo by Eric Flannery)

Chapter 11

Learning Goes With Earning

Coach Flannery has claimed more is to be learned from a loss than a win, but learning is at the forefront of everything Flannery teaches and is right up there with earning. *Earning* and *learning* have made St. Ed's into the successful program it has been, making it possible for student-athletes to become worthy of their jerseys.

With that in mind, he still realizes that he has had not only the personnel who have been good at learning as student-athletes but also ones who are talented at basketball.

Only those worthy enough will learn to make their next-play an improved effort. Often the game within the game, such as bad moments in a win, can be the foundation of learning opportunities.

"Every situation presents something to learn from," Coach Flannery said. "On the road, we're playing Beachwood and I am telling these guys what they need to do to win this game in the second half no matter what the score is. If we have that 10-0 lead and they come back, we have to learn from that. We won the game, but after the game I talked about the great job of getting off to that big start, but we have to keep that momentum going. We got flustered because of their crowd. Where's the leadership on the floor when the crowd is going crazy? Who's on the floor and settling things down? Even though we won that game (Beachwood), we take what we can and learn. Even when we win, we have to constantly be teaching."

After the game, Coach Flannery did not immediately see the silver lining in the loss to Shaker.

"I don't want to lose at any time," Coach Flannery said after the game. "This loss tells us that we cannot afford to play poorly. We learned something from that. If we make a run in the tournament, hopefully we learn from it."

Later the loss became a learning opportunity.

"I wouldn't admit it at the time, but by far it was the best thing that ever happened to us," Coach Flannery said later. "We had the ball with the chance to tie or win on the road against a very good team after we had played terribly. I walked out of there saying, 'We might have lost this game, but this team is pretty good.'"

With the loss to Shaker, the Eagles lost part of their identity, but with Funderburk out, others realized that their roles would change and they adapted accordingly.

"We had guys step up at that time (when D.J. was out)," Coach Nugent said. "Will took on more of a role. Mike became better. We don't want it to happen at that point, but we are excited as coaches to want to face that adversity. We lose to Shaker and now everybody in the area thinks they can beat us. One of the things they might have worried about St. Ed's was its length and athleticism. Losing D.J. Funderburk, we lost some of that length and athleticism. Now some of these teams may have been a little more confident. We were excited to see how our guys would respond to that."

On the flip side, games the Eagles won were also learning experiences, particularly the ones in which they jumped out to an early big lead and saw some of that advantage vanish later in the games such as at Beachwood.

"We were playing well enough that we got away with it," Coach Flannery said. "We were playing good basketball, and it was one of the worst things happening to our team in general. We were getting out to big leads, holding them and coasting. There were subtle messages in some of these games that teams were going to come back. The problem was that we were still winning those games. The kids were thinking, 'Ah, we get out to these big leads, we let them come back, and then we pulled away. We did what we had to do. We got the win.'

"This was the importance of what happened at Ignatius and Shaker. Even though we won at Ignatius, it was an overtime win and a game our guys felt lucky to win. To lose to Shaker the way we did really sent the message that we can't get away with doing that against really good teams. Those two games put a lot of meaning into what we really needed to do. It really helped me as a coach to keep these guys focused and to make sure that even if we got out to a great start, we had to keep it up. We got comfortable early in the season, saying 'Hey, we're pretty good; we don't need to play the full 32 minutes.'"

That's all part of the process of coaching and putting a team together. It goes back to the mind candy, and it goes back to everything Flannery's crew believes in as coaches.

"We talk it all we want, but we have to back it up by either the performances we have in games or the way we practice," Coach Flannery said. "There is the belief that no matter what the situation is, we are going to find a way. If we are not shooting the ball well, how are we going to win this game? Well, we are going to play great defense. We're going to shoot easy shots – get layups and free throws. We build that confidence constantly from the beginning to the middle to the end of the season."

That translated into the state championship game. The way this was going, it could have become frustrating. The student-athletes could have been discouraged. The coaches preached to them: it is going to be tough; it is going to be low scoring. They are going to have to play defense for 45 seconds at a time and they would have to play that way for 32 minutes.

The Eagles would learn that being down by six points with two minutes to go is nothing. They could do this. Take those examples and everything that happened throughout the year in games and practices and it's just a constant motivation the coaches were able to use. It was in the back of their minds that this situation might come up, so they had to remember this moment.

"I talked about the Shaker game to our guys," Coach Flannery said. "I said no matter how much I was disappointed that we lost, let's think about this. We finally got things together and played with a lot of energy and got some momentum. It was only a minute and a half. Let's learn from that. Let's understand that 1) we need to play that well all the time, and 2) if we are ever trailing by this much, we are able to make a quick run in a short period of time. Somewhere in the back of their heads it stuck."

It's easy to remove one's learning hat when winning because sometimes confidence can trot down that fine line into arrogance. Even coaches can slip into this mindset at times.

"Learning more from a loss than from a win is human nature," Coach Nugent said. "Sometimes it feels as if all we are doing is preaching. Nobody's really listening. We say, 'Guys, we are not really playing that well. We were fortunate enough to win.' We get comfortable and complacent. We don't feel as if we have to do what we did to get there. Then there is the obvious that comes out when we lose."

While St. Ed's players are taught to earn things to be worthy of the jersey, they are also taught to learn things, not just from practices and games, but also from off-court and off-season experiences. Coaches learn the same way.

"He's (Flannery) taught me so much," Coach Blanton said. "I learned so much from being a parent to being a coach. As a parent I could not see what a coach goes through every day. All I see is what is in front of me. All I see is the future. We see college and NBA. We don't see the small things that he sees, and he works his butt off for every day. He may spend three hours on something no one sees anywhere else. A parent can't see that. As a coach, I am able to see that."

Being on the third team or not making the team at all could be a learning experience. Coach Nugent played for Flannery while a junior at St. Ed's, but was cut his senior year. Yet he stayed on as the team's manager. The earning and learning has been a fruitful combination for him.

"As an 18- or 17-year old kid, it is a tough thing when I didn't make the team," Coach Nugent said. "Basketball has always been my passion. Coach Flannery was my neighbor at the time. One can fall into that complacent idea of 'here's my neighbor, here's a guy I have known my entire life and I just don't have to work as hard as I had the year previously; I have a spot. I was on the team my junior year; I'm going to make it automatically.' Life doesn't work that way. It was really tough but a good lesson for me to learn.

"Something I'll never forget is when I met with him; it was emotional. I was broken up about it, but he asked me at the end if I would like to stay on as a manager. He spun it to me this way. He said, 'Josh, I have always thought of you as someone who could be a coach. I think it would be great for you to stick around and learn how to coach. I would use you in ways that I wouldn't normally use a regular manager.' That was all I needed to hear because I loved being around the game. He was true to his word, too. He could have just said it and left me to be a typical manager."

The players learned from what was passed on to them through the strong tradition of basketball at St. Ed's.

"I think they started the tradition back then (in the 1990s)," Pisco said. "They had some great teams. We learned what Coach Flan had learned: that we had to put it all together to win the state championship this year. They were also good, but the most important thing is what we had learned from them."

The players had also learned from the loss and did not use it as a reason to give up, always thinking next play.

"In the game of basketball, someone can miss a shot and be pouting about it," Nichols said. "Then he can give up a layup on the other end because he didn't run back on defense. That can turn into something else. There are so many plays in basketball. We can't harp on what just happened -- like the Shaker game. I'm glad about what happened when it did happen. We could have hung our heads down and been sad about it and not moved on, but at the end of the day we had a greater goal, which was to win a state championship. That was one of our goals at the beginning of the season – to stay afloat and not think too much about what had just happened. We kept the main goal in mind."

Such is learning, next-play thinking, and laying claim to being worthy of the jersey.

Chapter 12

Flan's History as a Worthy Edsman

Eric Flannery was born in 1972 in Lakewood, Ohio as the youngest of the eight Flannery children of Jim and Judy.

He had three older brothers and four older sisters. As well as by being last in line, Flannery was removed from his siblings because eight years separated the first and seventh child and Flannery was three years younger than the next youngest, putting 11 years between him and the oldest.

Like their father James, Jim , Dan, Bryan and Eric all attended and graduated from St. Edward. All were athletic and played on several sports teams at the school.

The four sisters (Mary Lou, Kelly, Judi and Michelle), after graduating from St. James Grade School in Lakewood, split their high school years, two of them graduating from the Catholic, all-girls, Magnificat High School in Rocky River and two from the public Lakewood High School.

The sons of nearly all eight Baby-Boom Generation/GenX Flannerys have all attended or will attend St. Edward.

Although there was quite an age difference between Eric and his brothers, he still found a way to be involved in sports, particularly basketball, with his brothers and other boys in the neighborhood while growing up as a student at St. James.

"My oldest brother Jim, who now coaches with me, and I probably had the closest relationship," recalled Flannery. "It's different because he's the oldest and I'm the youngest. He was the one who was always around when I was."

The next oldest, Dr. Dan Flannery, was the "professional student" of the family and typically was not around when Eric was growing up in grade school. A 1980 graduate of St. Edward, Dr. Flannery went on to the University of Notre Dame, the alma mater of Jim Flannery, Sr., and The Ohio State University to do his undergraduate, master's and doctoral work while Eric was developing as a student-athlete basketball player and eventual coach.

Still Dr. Flannery and the other siblings had an impact on young Eric, who learned something from all of them that helped him to become a well-rounded teacher and coach.

"When I am being taken care of by a number of older brothers and sisters because of the wide range of the ages, I have varying relationships," Flannery said. "They definitely had an impact on me."

By the time Eric Flannery entered high school, Jim was already out of college and married with a family. Yet, he still had time to help continue the athletic relationship.

"He was the guy who was always playing one-on-one with me in the back," Eric said. "My high school years were basically playing basketball with him."

The Flannery boys had the advantage of having a unique man-made recreation center in their backyard, which served as a fine basketball court.

The boys were fortunate enough to have one big driveway between their house and their neighbor's. They actually shared the driveway. Then in the back, the driveway split out and there was a four-car garage. Two of the doors belonged to the Flannery family and two to the family next door.

"What was perfect is that it was shaped like the three-point line of a basketball court," Eric Flannery said. "We had lights on the garage. I could literally stay up in my yard and play basketball until 10 or 11 at night every day."

When his brothers were not around and none of the neighborhood boys were available, Flannery was not without basketball. Lack of teammates and opponents did not stop him. He would play games by himself, imagining games going on inside his head, as he played out the NBA finals or the collegiate Final Four.

"I played every NBA series by myself," Flannery explained. "I played every college basketball tournament by myself. I always had something going. I would write tournament brackets on the wall and I would play the LA Lakers against the Boston Celtics seven-game series, every single point, every single play in my head. That's how sick I was about basketball."

Competition and gamesmanship was a part of Flannery's life from day one.

"When I was growing up and when I got home from school, I would literally go in my backyard and play or play in my neighborhood until it got dark," Flannery said. "My childhood throughout grade school was going out and playing with the neighbors and having fun. That doesn't happen any longer, which is a shame.

"I loved it. I grew up in a great neighborhood with good kids. We played every sport and every game from Capture the Flag to Ghost in the Graveyard to Kick the Can. Then there were sports like basketball and football – you name it, we did it."

The lights on the garage and on the houses proved to be invaluable as well. If it were raining, Flannery would be outside playing basketball. If it snowed, he would shovel the back and play basketball. Flannery would play basketball a "ridiculous number" of hours, as he described it.

While Jim as the oldest was the biggest moral support for Eric as the youngest, it was Bryan Flannery who had the most athletic influence and inspiration on Eric.

Bryan was the biggest of the Flannery boys. He was a senior at St. Edward High School when Eric was an eighth grader at St. James, so they just missed being in high school together.

While he also played on the basketball team at St. Ed's for then Head Coach Jim Slatinsky, Bryan Flannery's primary sport at St. Edward was football. He played on the Eagle football teams for the late Al O'Neill, graduating in 1986.

"My brother Bryan was the brother I looked up to and lived in the shadows of because he had a very successful athletic career," Eric said.

At St. Ed's Bryan was an all-state at defensive tackle for the 9-1 Eagles in 1985. He was able to earn a scholarship to Notre Dame, the alma mater of his father and brother and parent school of St. Ed's.

Although he did wind up at Notre Dame, it wasn't a direct path there. Bryan was recruited by Michigan and Ohio State and was offered scholarships to both schools. He wanted to go to Notre Dame; however, he was not recruited by then Fighting Irish Head Coach Gerry Faust.

"Bryan was the best athlete in the family because he had the size; he was 6-3 and athletic," Eric Flannery said. "He would dominate in grade school and was good in high school. He always dreamed about playing football at Notre Dame.

"Earle Bruce from Ohio State and Bo Schembechler from Michigan came to our house. Those schools offered him scholarships, but he always wanted to go to Notre Dame. Gerry Faust was out of a job at Notre Dame after Bryan's senior year in high school. When Coach Lou Holtz got the job, my brother sent a letter to Coach Holtz and he invited him up to Notre Dame with my dad. Watching game films, Coach Holtz offered my brother a scholarship on his visit. My brother recruited Notre Dame, and he wound up fulfilling his dream of attending Notre Dame."

Flannery started at defensive tackle on Coach Holtz's 1988 national championship team.

"I spent many of my high school years traveling to Notre Dame with my family to watch Bryan play," Eric said. "I was watching football games with my family on Saturdays and Sundays. He (Bryan) provided a lot of inspiration athletically. He was the guy who made me realize I could do almost anything I want.

"Here's my brother at Notre Dame playing on the national championship team. It was inspirational just to witness it. It was neat to see how sports brought the family together, all the travelling for the weekends and going to parties. That was probably my first big experience as to how influential sports could be on somebody."

Bryan Flannery took his success from student-athletics and had a fine career as a politician. Bryan was state congressman in the Ohio House of Representatives 1999-2002. In 2003 his district was consolidated with another.

Never one to give up, Bryan ran for Ohio governor in 2006, losing in the Democratic primary to Ted Strickland, who eventually became the governor as predecessor to current Ohio Governor John Kasich.

While his brothers were influential in terms of athletics, Eric Flannery's sisters were strong influences on him academically and socially.

"Going back to those relationships, my sisters are still very close," Eric Flannery said. "They were all good to me."

Eric Flannery himself played on the CYO (Catholic Youth Organization) teams at St. James. "Back then CYO was the thing," Flannery said. "Nowadays there are so many other options. We joined the Lakewood Recreation League, and I would ride my bike up to Lakewood High School. We played games forever. My mom and dad never went to any games. We coached ourselves."

Simply put, parents just were not involved in a student-athlete's activities as much as they are today. It simply was a boys'-only club.

Flannery also rode his bike to the baseball fields, where he would play ball. That's how they grew up in the 1960s, '70s and '80s.

"We did it on our own and we made a lot of friends," Flannery said. "We got a lot of exercise. Kids are now playing video games. It exposed us to a lot of different things. Our generation benefited from that. We were able to make good and bad decisions growing up and learn from them. We were able to build a lot of relationships through that. I am not sure that today kids get that same experience."

While organized sports provided some opportunities, they weren't enough for Flannery, who took advantage of that backyard.

"I had friends," Flannery said. "I still had the one-on-one, two-on-two, three-on-three games, but when no one was around I was doing it myself. My own kids don't understand this. I would come home from school at 4 o'clock, and I would be out there until 10 o'clock at night, just shooting baskets in my back yard. If it were raining, I would have mud all over my hands because of the dirt. My hands would be soaked. My body would be soaked."

When winter came, the weather conditions, elements and after effects did not faze the young Flannery.

"I played on the ice," he recalled. "I remember shoveling and not being able to get it all up on to the lawn and the ice would be there and

I would be sliding around. I had on gloves. I always loved basketball. I enjoyed and loved other sports, but for some reason, I always had that affiliation with basketball."

The CYO teams at St. James played in the West Suburban League against such schools as St. Christopher, St. Brendan, St. Bernadette, St. Raphael, and St. Richard.

Playing basketball in his head, while acting out his thoughts on the court, prepared him to grasp the mental part of the game, setting himself up to be a coach, and taking on the insurmountable task of the psychology of the game.

In the fall of 1986, Coach Flannery entered St. Edward High School as a freshman. He was continuing the family legacy that his father and three brothers had set before him. Before he was finished, he would play on four interscholastic sports teams: football, baseball, basketball and golf.

After playing nose tackle on the freshman and JV football teams, he gave up football after his sophomore year and took up golf instead so that he could go with his family to South Bend, Ind. and watch his brother play for Notre Dame on Saturdays.

He kept up with baseball and basketball as both would later be experiences that he could transfer into his coaching career.

The Eagles were decent in the 1980s under coaches such as Buck Riley, Jim Slatinsky, and Mike Kearns, but nothing exceptional. This changed in Flannery's junior year of 1988-89, when the Eagles won the Lorain Admiral King District championship and went on to the regional in Canton under Kearns. It was quite a feat since it had been more than 20 years since a Cuyahoga County team last made it out of the now-defunct Admiral King district.

After backyard basketball, Flannery and friends had a thing called RBA, which was (Rocky) River Basketball Association. It was one court. It started out as KBA, Kensington Basketball Association. These were similar to the legendary playgrounds and public parks of the New York Rucker Leagues.

His indoctrination to KBA came when he was in high school and his brother took him up to Kensington Grade School in Rocky River. It was a basketball court next to the grade school. They went there after school and had to get in line to play. They had to get their own team of four players.

"It was four-on-four, full-court basketball," Flannery said. "Barry Clemens, who played for the Cavs, was there and all these older guys were there playing basketball. We would simply put our teams together or put our names on the list and wait for our turns."

KBA was run by Mike McLaren, who had a big, long beard.

"We went up to KBA, and there would be unbelievable games," Flannery recalled. "First we were on the court. If we won, we stayed on. If we lost, we got off the court. We could have waited another half hour, 45 minutes, an hour, or two hours to play. It depended upon how badly someone wanted to play. I met a lot of people and made some friends."

When KBA shut down, they moved it to the Rocky River Recreation Center behind the police station. They changed the name to RBA and they had two full courts instead of one.

"It was just Mike McLaren who would go to these courts and organize the names on the list, and we would wait for our turn," Flannery said. "The games just kept getting better and better."

These kinds of student-athletic opportunities fueled the St. Ed's-St. Ignatius rivalry, which is one of the most unique rivalries in the entire country. It was and continues to be so intense in basketball and in other sports because the student-athletes not only get together during summers and after school but attend many of the same Catholic grade schools before entering one of the two high schools.

Flannery had a group of friends who went to Ignatius. Friends of Flannery were St. Ignatius products such as Kevin Neitzel, Ryan Spicer, Dave McNamee and Chris Fletcher. Neitzel went on to play college basketball at John Carroll. Spicer also played cornerback on the St. Ignatius football teams that began a dynasty in 1988 that extended into the 2010s as they won 11 state championships. Spicer went on to Ohio Wesleyan

"I played against them when they were at Ignatius," Flannery said. "Spicer, Fletcher and Neitzel were three of my good friends. The four of us grew a bond through that. We played a lot together. We started in high school and played through college and a few years after that."

The four of them would enter the Hoop it Up and Gus Macker tournaments.

"They were some pretty competitive, high-spirited games," Flannery said. "There had been an article, a little blurb, about a Gus Macker Tournament. It had a reference to our team being the Mark Price brothers. We were a bunch of 6-foot White guys shooting threes, and we beat a team made up of Division I college players in the finals to win the tournament.

"We had those types of runs while I grew up on basketball. Everything from growing up in the neighborhoods to going to places like KBA and RBA and getting together with my buddies and playing in tournaments."

Basketball was one way to build relationships, but Flannery found other ways as well.

During his junior season at St. Edward, Flannery was attending a St. Ed's hockey game at Winterhurst Ice Rink, now renamed Serpentini-Winterhurst Arena.

He was with a group of friends who met at the game with a group of girls from Magnificat High School, the all-girls school in nearby Rocky River. While there, Flannery noticed a girl named Lori Szucs, whom he had never seen before prior to this night, but he did know some of the girls in the group. While Flannery was a junior, Szucs was a sophomore.

"I could remember like it was yesterday," Flannery recalled. "I didn't know this one girl and I thought, man, she is pretty good looking. After the hockey game, my group of friends met up with her group of friends. I asked one of the girls whom I knew, 'Who is that?' She said it is Lori Szucs."

Then Lori approached Coach Flannery and said, "Can I get your friend's phone number?" So Coach Flannery was introduced to his future wife by her asking him for his best friend's phone number.

"That was the first time I talked to her," he said. "She liked my friend or thought my friend was good looking. Of course, I said, 'I don't have it,' as if I don't have my best friend's phone number. That was my first interaction. I thought she was this attractive girl, and she came up to me asking for my best friend's phone number."

They became friends after that first night of meeting. They did a few things with the groups but didn't date the first six or seven months of their relationship.

"During those first six or seven months of the relationship, I wanted to date her," Flannery said. "I did pursue as often as I could, but we became just good friends. We talked on the phone and built a good relationship that way. One day the light clicked on in her head and she realized what a great looking guy I was and what a wonderful person I was and she asked if we might start dating."

So while he was playing out his high school basketball career, he was dating Lori Szucs during his spare time. The emotional support from his girlfriend helped carry him through to graduation.

He graduated as one of few student-athletes ever to play on a district championship basketball team, yet a St. Ed's team had still never made it to the state final four.

Prior to his graduation in his junior season, the Eagles upset two state-ranked teams in Lorain Admiral King and Lorain Senior in the districts to win it. The team then lost in the regional tournament to Jackson Township from the Massillon area. To be the first team in school history to win a district title and cut down the nets was special, yet the young Flannery found it unsettling that it was the first time for a school that had been standing since 1949.

His experiences were enough for him to be the complete student-athlete at St. Ed's. He became the fifth Flannery to graduate from St. Ed's. Following Dad Jim in '56; were Jim Jr. in '79; Dr. Dan in '80; Bryan in '86; and Eric in '90.

With a decent enough student-athletic career at St. Edward, Eric Flannery set off to college to study and play Division III college basketball at Penn State-Behrend in the fall of 1990.

He didn't quite have the size to play Division I college basketball and none had offered him any kind of scholarships, but schools like Penn State-Behrend did show an interest.

Although he wanted to extend his playing life in basketball, eventually he became interested in becoming a coach and found the small-college setting to be too isolated.

"After being at Penn Sate-Behrend a few weeks, I became homesick and didn't like it," Flannery said. "Division III college basketball is tough. A student-athlete has to be with it all the time academically and play a sport full time. A student-athlete has to be really committed. I decided to come home and was thinking of transferring to John Carroll. I would decide later if I wanted to play basketball or not."

Flannery opted against John Carroll and instead matriculated to Cleveland State. Although he did not play basketball at the Division I CSU, it proved to be an invaluable time for him. During his six years as a student at Cleveland State, Flannery held every basketball coaching position at St. Ed's except one. He was the assistant freshman coach, head freshman coach, assistant JV coach, head JV coach, assistant varsity coach, and top varsity assistant to an interim coach. It was quite a path to becoming a head coach -- almost like working for IBM, coming in as a file clerk and ending up being CEO after going through all the steps.

Because it worked for him, he has the right to instruct young students now who want to go into coaching and can tell them that they don't necessarily have to be a collegiate student-athlete to become a coach. A perpetual "internship" at one's old high school could work just as well.

However, if someone wants to play Division III ball and isn't using the experience to transform into a coach, he welcomes that desire and will do whatever he can to get his student-athletes playing situations.

"There are a couple things to that," Flannery said. "I can use the experience I had and advise my players about college. I have a lot of Division III-type players who go through here. My advice to them is 'you really have to love it if you want to play Division III college basketball.'"

He tells them that they are going to be putting more time into basketball, but school is going to be harder, and they are going to start thinking about their career or future.

"I tell them my story; I say, 'Listen, I went away to play college basketball but realized I wasn't going to play professionally,'" he continued. "You come at a crossroads where you have to make a decision. 'Am I going to hang on to this?' one asks. I could have played four years of college basketball and had a great time doing it. Part of me regrets that I should have gone to Carroll and played."

If he would have, we don't know if it would have worked out the same way, but hopefully it would have. What he does know is that the turn he took at the time was the right one.

"I was happy that it did work out the way it did," Flannery said. "When I was in high school, I never thought about being a coach. Then when I went away and came home I was still thinking that I was going to be a player by transferring to John Carroll or Baldwin Wallace."

Instead he went in a different direction.

His dad was an accountant and nobody else in his family was an accountant. So, as the youngest, his first inclination was to be an accountant like his dad and do what he did and to make him proud.

"I could carry on his legacy of being an accountant," Flannery said.

He enrolled in Cleveland State and took two accounting courses right away and failed miserably at both of them.

"I did poorly," he said. "Honest to God, I think I finished one class and got a D and the other class I dropped. It was too hard. I just couldn't do it."

Since he needed to find a way to pay for his education, he also worked in a factory downtown, Cleveland Oak Belting, a company that cut break shoes and belting and lining. He worked from 6 a.m. to early afternoon.

"I was making money and taking a couple courses at Cleveland State," Flannery said.

He wasn't necessarily a full-time student. While he was taking some classes, Kearns, the head basketball coach at St. Ed's, asked him if he wanted to help coach the freshman basketball team. Now he was doing three things: working in a factory, taking classes, and helping out as an assistant coach.

"So I coached and at that point I realized that this is something I might like to do," Flannery explained. "I'm working in a factory and I said to myself that I don't think I want to work in a factory the rest of my life. I could still be involved in sports and maybe I should try this coaching thing."

That first year he was the assistant freshman basketball coach, Flannery was asked by Mike Girimont, the baseball coach at the time, if he would like to help coach baseball. He became the JV baseball coach at 18 years old. He was coaching and enjoying it.

"I enjoyed the coaching part of baseball," he said. "Here I am coaching, dealing with the kids, and I am having a good time and I am not 'working.'"

Although he saw coaching as more fun than "work," he was still working in the factory. The next year came and he decided that this was where he wanted to go. He wanted to become a teacher and a coach.

"I said, 'All right, I am going to change my major to education,'" said Flannery of his next move. "Since I was in accounting, I thought let's try math. I was going to be a math teacher. So at Cleveland State, I go to my first couple math classes and the first teacher was foreign; I couldn't understand a word she said. The other teacher was in a class of 200. She had a microphone on and was about 85 years old, and I couldn't understand what she was saying."

At that time at Cleveland State, students simply showed up to math class and took tests. That was it. That was the class.

"We didn't have chances to talk to the teacher," Flannery said. "We basically listened to the teacher and took math tests at a testing site. That's how they did the first classes. I basically flunked out of math. I was terrible. I started my college career doing poorly. I was failing or getting D's or dropping classes. I was really questioning where I was going to go."

After bombing out of both math and accounting, Flannery was left with one question: "What am I going to do?"

It's no secret that labor-related/blue-collar jobs do offer two things: job security and decent money.

"They liked me (at the factory)," Coach Flannery said. "I was working hard. They were trying to promote me there. Even though I was 19 or 20, they were giving me delivery jobs. They were trying to take me into different positions. They were asking me what I would like to do with their company. So I was doing that, making some money, and still coaching."

It took Flannery six years to graduate from Cleveland State. During that time he was trying to still decide what he wanted to do. At some point during that second year at CSU he went from assistant freshman to assistant JV coach. Kearns had left, and Girimont became the new head coach for basketball as well as baseball at St. Ed's. Because Flannery realized that coaching was what he wanted to do through his promotion at St. Ed's, and because he really loved it, he started gaining some direction.

Leading into his third year of college, a new head coach at St. Ed's, Tim Schmotzer, arrived and asked Flannery to be the head freshman coach. He said yes and before even graduating from college, he was getting his first head basketball coaching experience. He was still coaching baseball. The factory thing started to fade as he got more into coaching.

"I said physical education is probably where a coach should get his degree, so I enrolled in the Physical Education Department," Flannery said. "From there I got my major."

After Tim Schmotzer named him the head freshman coach, a position Flannery kept for one year, he became the head JV coach. He held four spots in four years. Since the climb up the ladder was a smooth and fast one, Flannery decided to go for all the marbles – the head coaching job. Schmotzer left and took the North Olmsted head job, and Flannery applied for the job.

"I felt pretty good about myself," Flannery said. "I just found it the other day, a rejection letter from St. Ed's. In 1994 I was 22 years old and applied for the job and didn't get it. I was cocky; I thought I knew what I was doing. I probably thought I deserved the job."

He was still going to school and trying to get his degree. Greg Zimmerman came in to be the head coach, and he asked Flannery to continue as the head JV coach. That was for one year. Zimmerman and the school severed ties halfway through his second year -- about 10 games into the '95-'96 season.

Pete Novakovic became the interim head coach. Although, Novakovic might have had more overall experience in coaching, Flannery still had a pulse on the St. Ed's community, because he had been with the program longer.

"Pete was one of the greatest assistants that I knew," Flannery said. "He was just a friendly, outgoing, good person. He was here for only two months. He was named an assistant coach just that year. That year they made Pete the interim coach and I was the assistant coach."

Now Flannery moved up to assistant varsity coach, or top assistant to the interim head coach, halfway through the year. That year, the Eagles had three really good sophomores, Steve Logan, Sam Clancy, and Steve Lepore, whom Flannery had coached on the JV team the previous year.

They also had a junior, Gino Bartolone, who would go on to a fine collegiate career at Kentucky Wesleyan, where he played in four national championship games, and another sophomore in Pete Latkovic.

"At this point, we knew the program was turning," Coach Flannery said about the program as it was beginning its huge upswing. "We lost maybe five or six games during that season, but really started playing well toward the end of that year."

They upset Cleveland Heights and Glenville, both ranked in the top three in the state, in the regional at Cleveland State. The team in the year (1995-96) before Flannery fully took over ended up going to the final four for the first time in the school's history.

The Eagles lost to LaSalle in the final four in a close game, a game they probably should have won. The core of the team was made up of sophomores, so the next season they had almost the whole team coming back. The head coaching job opened up when the season was over.

"They had an eight-person committee when I sat down," Flannery recalled. "I was happy to get the interview. They were at a table and it was pretty intense. Jack Brindza was the athletic director back then, so he conducted it. A football coach and some alumni were on the committee. It was a pretty intense interview. I wasn't sure I was going to get it."

Between 60 and 70 people applied for the job. With the team making it to the final four with a core group of sophomores the year before, it was an attractive post to many. The program had a lot of young talent. Pete Novakovic, who was the interim head coach, also applied for it.

"We were both in an uncomfortable position," Coach Flannery said. "We both had our part in the final-four team and were applying for the same job the following year. He put his support behind me if he didn't get it and I did him. I said, 'If I don't get it, I hope you do' and vise-versa."

Jim Kubacki, who was the principal at the time and who is now the president of the high school, called Flannery and offered him the job.

"I just remembered the phone call," Flannery said. "I was still living at home with my parents."

Mr. Kubacki in his phone conversation said that the school wanted to go with one of its own.

"I hope you would be interested in being the head coach at St. Ed's," Kubacki said.

Flannery did not hesitate.

"I was excited to say the least," he recalled. "Here I am at 23, going to be 24 soon, and I was going to be the head coach at my alma mater and be in a position in which we know we are going to be pretty good. It's a pretty neat, unique thing how it worked out."

When the job opened up, the players lobbied for Flannery. They gathered around and met with Kubacki. They wanted him to be the head coach the following year.

"That could be good or bad," Flannery admitted. "'Awe, they just want this guy because he's nice and maybe he's a pushover,' some might have thought. It could hurt someone sometimes, but they really went to bat for me and wanted me to be the head coach. They saw what type of coach I could be if I were the head coach."

The school wanted to go with someone who would be at the school for a while. They wanted someone who was going to stabilize the program. There had been a lot of turnaround and not much success. When Flannery played back in '89, the Eagles had won the district championship, the first one in the school's history. There wasn't much basketball history at the school. As it was to turn out, Flannery has been a part of all the district championship teams, either as a player or as a coach.

"It is just a lot of things like that that just turned out well for me," Flannery said.

So St. Ed's took a chance on a 24-year-old head coach to build a program that was already on an upswing but which had been very unstable in its coaching ranks. Flannery's sincerity made a difference. The St. Ed's administration and selection committee were sold on the idea that this would be his dream job and consequently he would turn out some good things for the school. The number of good things might not have been anticipated.

"I said, 'Hey, I am a St. Ed's guy,'" Flannery said in his interview. "'My dad went here. My older brothers went here. This is my dream job. This is where I want to be. Can I guarantee that I will be here in five, 10, 20 years? I have no idea what is going to happen and neither could an older person. I can guarantee you this: this is where I want to be and this is my ultimate destination. This is my dream job and you're giving me the opportunity to coach my dream job. If I could, I would I stay here forever. That's my plan.' That's what I sold them on and what I believed.

"I had no illusions of coaching in college. I just had the illusion of winning a state championship with this team right now. This is what I want to do: be the head basketball coach at St. Edward High School. I wasn't thinking about what I wanted to do when I would be 30 or 35. Maybe that's why I am still here. At that time this was it. 'You're going out looking for people you want. You have to start looking at people who want this, who want to be here. You will at least know that if I do or don't win a state championship in '96, '97, or '98 that I still want to be here.' I want to be the coach, this is my home and this is my school."

This was the job he would cherish, and that's what separated him from most of the other coaches. This wasn't just a guy who wanted to win with these players and then leave. This was a person who wanted to build a program. Whether he would or wouldn't, he wanted to stay at the school.

To this day, Flannery admits that if Novakovic would have received the job, he probably would have wanted to stay as an assistant, because he loved the school.

"There was a much better chance of my staying and helping him than vice-versa," Flannery said.

Novakovic wound up coaching somewhere else. There were guys with Flannery at the time. Pete Campbell was on staff and still is. St. Ed's had only one freshman team at the time. He had only a few men coaching. His staff has grown to 15 gentlemen.

Things just seemed to fall into place for Coach Flannery as he was developing into the head coach at St. Ed's, with all the promotions he had enjoyed during his six years as a student at Cleveland State.

Flannery continued dating Lori Szucs throughout college. With the head coaching position secure by the summer of 1996, Flannery and Szucs married on July 20, 1996.

Part of the reason Flannery returned home from Penn State-Behrend in 1990 was that he missed Lori, who was still in high school when he began college and she missed him. Lori was to return the favor a year later when she started out at Kent State to study interior design and after a month returned to the Cleveland area to enroll in Cuyahoga County

Community College East to pursue the same studies.

While she was living with mutual friends who attended John Carroll University, Lori stayed in a house right across from Cleveland Heights High School. While she was going to Tri-C East, Flannery was living at home and working in the factory. They would see each other a couple times a week. They kept the relationship going through college and were getting serious.

"We knew at the age of 20 or 21 that we were probably going to get married," Flannery recalled. "In '95 after we went out to dinner, I drove her to Winterhurst since that was the site of the first time I met her. I proposed on the bench outside of Winterhurst Arena."

In dating Flannery during part of his playing days and during his assistant coaching career, Lori Szucs, now Lori Flannery, knew what she was getting into by marrying him. With the odd hours coaches and anyone involved in student-athletics must invest in their careers, a wife also has to live with these odd hours. This would mean nights and weekends tied up with basketball. It had been new to her when the whole courtship began back in 1989, but she quickly learned to be a supportive basketball wife.

"I have to say, I was not a very athletic person growing up," Lori Flannery said. "I never played basketball. Even when we were dating in high school and he played, I still don't think I really knew much. We were in high school, so I didn't care."

Lori Flannery grew up in the West Park area of Cleveland, attended St. Pat's Grade School and started out at St. Joseph Academy during her freshman year of high school before transferring to Magnificat at the beginning of her sophomore year. She had played some on the volleyball teams at St. Pat's and St. Joe's.

Coming from a mostly non-athletic family, Lori transformed into being part of a highly athletic family. She had one sister who was older, but she never played any sports. Lori did summer baseball, but she didn't see it as really competitive.

"I was laughing when I was talking to Sean the other night and he was asking me if we ever could take dance lessons," Lori Flannery said. "I said, 'Sean, we're not really that kind of family. We're just sports. We stick to that.' It's not that we don't like any of that stuff; it is just what we know."

Lori Flannery has learned to make basketball a family affair and a social event. It's simply what they do on weekends during the winters. Coach Flannery said he could probably count on one hand the number of St. Ed's games Lori has missed attending during the past 18 years.

"His being at St. Ed's is a unique experience," Lori explained. "I am not sure it would be like this if he were somewhere else. Being at St. Ed's is what makes it good. When the kids were babies, we always went to games. If we wanted to see Eric and spend time with him, we went to a game. If we weren't willing to do those things, we were not going to see him on the weekends. During the week he would get home right before bed time."

When they were first married, they lived in a tiny one-bedroom apartment in a house owned by one of his sisters in Cleveland. The apartment had one small area outside of the bedroom and a tiny bathroom. They decided to live there once he started his job as a physical education and health teacher and then when they started making money, they would look for a bigger place. They lived there for a month or two. Later they luckily found a place in Lakewood, renting half of a double on Atkins.

"We ended up buying the double as our first purchase a few years into our marriage and working lives," Coach Flannery said.

Both of their sons, Sean and P.J., were born while they were living in the house on Atkins. Then Lori became pregnant with Grace, their third child and first daughter. Since they were expanding, they needed a little more room. They wanted to get another house.

Since Lori had grown up in West Park, she always wanted to live in the quaint neighborhood of Cleveland as an adult. In 2001, they bought a house on Marquis in West Park across from St. Joe's.

"It was a tiny house but the only thing we could afford back then," Coach Flannery said. "We had great neighbors and a great neighborhood."

So they lived in the West Park house with three children and soon realized the house was getting small.

"We had to make a choice; we either had to move or put an addition on the house," Coach Flannery recalled. "For us, it was cheaper to move.

We were looking and fortunate to find a house in Westlake."

They picked up and moved to Westlake in 2003 and then found themselves expecting their fourth child and second daughter. Abbey was born in 2004. With all these things going on, Flannery was coaching and teaching but also making a private-school income.

Two months prior to St. Ed's winning the state championship for the first time in 1998, Sean Flannery was born. It was fitting and somewhat ironic that Sean was on the second team to win the state championship in 2014.

While he was practicing with the JV team every day from November to February during his freshman year and with both the varsity and JV teams during the 2013-14 seasons, Sean Flannery's participation in St. Ed's had begun much earlier.

"One time I had to go to a doctor's appointment or something and I had nobody to watch Sean," Lori said. "He was about a month old if that. I had to drop him off at St. Ed's in his car seat. I put him on the stage (behind the north basket in the Eagles' Nest) so Eric could watch him while his practice was going on and I was at a doctor's appointment. Sean was already into it at a month old."

The other three children have also come to enjoy the basketball life even though at times they might prefer to be doing something else.

"It wasn't always easy especially when my kids went through different phases in their lives," Lori explained. "The girls don't always want to go to games. They will give me a hard time, like, 'We have to go to another game?' Even when my son was in eighth grade he started giving me a hard time. I said, 'Put a smile on your face and get in the car.' We just work through it and we are all together."

Sean began attending St. Ed's in 2012, and P.J. began in 2014. With the boys as student-athletes at the school, it has become even more of an event, meshing the Flannery family with the St. Ed's family.

"With Sean there, it is special," Lori said. "It hasn't been easy, but we've all learned that this is our life. We accept it and we do enjoy it. There are things my kids have been able to do and see that they might not appreciate now, but when they get older they might look back on this time and realize it has been pretty cool."

While being in the St. Ed's basketball fold, Lori has been the woman behind the man whose teams have won 340 games.

"Winning makes everything more fun," Lori said. "Being in a special program and being around these kids with their high goals always makes it more pleasant. This year (2014) was especially a blast. We had some years that weren't so great. We take the good with the bad."

Lori was working in interior design at the time they were engaged, but Coach Flannery still had his student teaching to do. The day he signed the contract to be the head coach was a very exciting day for Lori.

"She is by far the best," Coach Flannery said of Lori. "She does a lot of extra duties and has a son on the team. Just the simple support of me and the team makes her great. It takes a special person to be a coach's wife."

Lori has been an essential part of Flannery's coaching career for 24 years counting the years he was an assistant coach.

"When I came back home from school I started coaching right away," Coach Flannery said. "She knew that this is what I wanted to do. She understood that I was not going to be an accountant. We had practices and games. Right away she was very supportive. She tries to be at everything. She loves the kids on the team. St. Ed's basketball has been intertwined with everything we have done since we have been together in high school."

Coach Flannery certainly has the intelligence and competitiveness to be successful in more lucrative work areas than private school education.

"It would be easy to say let's go find something else with a better retirement with more money and make it easier, but he wouldn't be happy and be where he loves," Lori said. "He could be offered a job that he could not possibly pass up, an opportunity of a lifetime, but he loves St. Ed's so much."

In addition to support, Lori does things many other parents do, like serving the pre-game meals and assembling scrapbooks for the team at the end of the season.

Chapter 13

Flannery and USA Basketball

Tim Flannery, Coach Flannery's uncle, attended St. Edward briefly as a youth and was the athletic director at nearby North Olmsted High School in the 1980s, where he ran a fine athletic program that housed powerful boys' and girls' soccer programs. . Tim Flannery later went on to a fine career at the National Federation of State High School Athletic Associations in Indianapolis.

Many of the soccer players who played their prep ball at NOHS were members of the East-West Soccer Club and its offshoot organization, the East-West Ambassadors. East-West became well known for initiating what became known as *athletic diplomacy*. Soccer student-athletes, and later baseball student-athletes, would not only go to dozens of countries to play sports but also serve as youth ambassadors for the United States.

East-West became so renowned for what it did that when its traveling group would leave the country, it would first stop at the White House for photo opportunities with various Presidents. The White House supported these efforts because those in charge of the U.S. realized how important it was for youth to build good relations with other countries and one of the best ways of doing that was through sports.

Although he wasn't quite planning on it, Coach Flannery has had similar athletic diplomacy missions while working with youth around the country. He has been involved with USA Basketball, the national development program that also prepares youth teams for international competition, for the past 14 years.

"Fourteen years ago, in 2000, my uncle Tim nominated me as a representative to the coaches of the national federation," Coach Flannery said. "He nominated me among a group of other coaches. I was chosen to be on a committee."

Although a committee person does not actually coach, his job is to name the coaches and the players, putting the teams together. It was Flannery's job to get to know student-athletes and recommend personnel. Every summer he would fly out to Colorado and watch these players work. If they needed to put together a team for competition, it was his job along with five other gentlemen to do it and to name the coaches. He did that for 12 years.

Each nomination would be a four-year commitment. After his first four years expired, they asked him to return for four more years, which took him through 2009. Since one is not allowed to serve more than two consecutive terms, his committee duties were done.

"I was hoping that maybe at that time I could do some coaching," Coach Flannery said. "One is not allowed to coach while being a committee person. I could still make a name for myself."

So they revised the rules and asked him to come back again as a committee person. As a result, he served three consecutive terms as a committee person. However, in 2010 a special circumstance arose involving the Youth Olympic Games. It was the first-ever Youth Olympic Games in which they were recruiting high school youth to compete in Olympic events. They invited them to Singapore.

"They asked me, someone they knew and trusted, if I wanted to go with the 3-on-3 team to Singapore," Coach Flannery said. "That's how I got to coach the first 3-on-3 team ever."

Then his four-year term for the committee expired again in 2012 so they asked him to coach. His first year as a coach, coaching the U-16, U-17 team, was 2013. The coaching is only a two-year commitment. Since he did it in 2013 and in 2014, in theory, he is finished with his commitment.

"If they ask me to coach or do something else, then I'll go again," Coach Flannery said.

The international experience had been something far from his mind when he started coaching at St. Ed's. He liked familiar grounds; but once the program had gone national and he had gone national with USA Basketball, he thought, "Why not go international?" So he did.

"I never intended or had a reason to leave this country for any purpose whatsoever," Coach Flannery said. "I never had any thoughts in my head that I wanted to be this world traveler or visit other countries. I like to be at home. There are things in the United States I haven't seen yet that I would rather go see. USA basketball has opened my borders. It has been an unbelievable experience for me, but something that I am trying to do to make me a better coach and make our program a better program."

Athletic diplomacy became a big part of his experience with USA Basketball, which he was able to carry over to his team and allow his own St. Ed's players to function more diplomatically.

"That's the international experience," Coach Flannery said. "When I walk the streets with these kids in Singapore, they have 'USA' on their chests. They are 6-8 and 6-10 players and people know they play basketball. They are stopped and asked for their autographs. I feel a sense of representation – I am representing the USA here. I had better be on my best behavior, and I had better be doing a good job. People may never see another American citizen in their lives or this might be their first impression of what the USA is all about and here I am being that person."

He learned ambassadorship and diplomacy early. His late dad was a state representative and city councilman. His brother was a state representative and ran for governor.

"Politics is in our blood," Coach Flannery said. "I always say that I hate politics. I never really did like it when I was helping my brother, but the reality is that I am in politics. I am in politics with the parents, the school and everything I do. I'm making connections. I'm dealing with a lot of people from a lot of backgrounds. I'm representing the school. I'm dealing with alumni. I'm basically selling myself and selling my school. It is politics."

This has helped Flannery be one of the most cooperative coaches with the media around the Cleveland area and by extension around the state. He is always available for interviews, answers questions lucidly and eloquently, and makes his players available for interviews.

"I don't understand people who don't (cooperate with the media)," Coach Flannery said. "I will say this. I think all coaches have egos. This is why we coach. I want people to like me. That's my ego, but I also want what's best for my kids. If someone from the media wants to talk or has a question, I view it as I am helping these kids while I am helping myself and my program. Once in a while it is negative or time consuming, but if I can help one of my players get some attention, then I am going to do it.

"Look at USA Basketball. People might not know it, but the same people I deal with in USA basketball are the same guys who deal with the NBA and the colleges. So the guys who ask Mike Krzyzewski to coach the USA Olympic team or Chuck Daly or Billy Donovan to coach the U-19 team are the same guys who are talking to me. It's not like there's 500 people out in Colorado running USA Basketball. USA Basketball is run by about four or five people."

In Colorado, they know he is going to work well with the other coaches and the youth, and he in turn knows that the respect is mutual.

"Obviously, when putting together teams and bringing people in, we don't know what we are getting," Coach Flannery said. "They might hear that this guy is a great coach and he has had great teams, but when they bring that person in, he might be a hothead. He might be someone who doesn't represent USA Basketball well. He makes bad decisions or thinks it is all about him. I try not to be that way. They tell me what to do and I do it."

He has learned many things from USA basketball.

"It's probably not as crazy as one might think; basketball is not rocket science," Coach Flannery said. "As far as the X's and O's go, it is one of the biggest things I've learned. We would use what we call a European ball screen offense. There are a couple different pressures and traps that I've learned through USA basketball and through other coaches. I could look back and say, 'If I only knew this when I had this team and run this offense, we would have been a lot better.' I think that is all part of the coaching process. Now I have to see if I can use it appropriately for what I have going forward.

"Some people can learn these things just by watching videos. I am just fortunate enough to live it. I can ask questions while we are doing it and see it implemented first hand. There are drills that I use that I have learned from this experience that maybe other people haven't seen. It might make me a better coach or it might make my players a little better."

At USA Basketball, he is getting a chance to watch, to do, to help, to coach, and to implement on his own. It is almost like a whole other season even though it is condensed and short term. He is helping a team prepare for a tournament or a world competition. He's getting a crash course on how to put a team together, even though it is not similar to high school with a five-month period, dragging out practices.

"It's almost like a coaches' clinic on steroids," he said. "I'm getting some of the best coaches around the country and around the world in a short period of time versus watching clinics and educating myself. I can even experiment with it. It is another level of learning."

For someone who is so big on learning and earning, this experience has been channeled into his own career as a coach.

"I think the full USA experience has made me a better coach by being around other coaches and around good coaches," Flannery said. "Any experience, good or bad, helps make me a better person. All my experiences with USA Basketball have been mostly positive. I pick up something new, such as mind candy or how to deal with a person/player. When I make these connections and someone from California or Utah sees that the coach from St. Ed's is coaching the USA team, it brings out the name St. Ed's."

It brings out that national recognition little by little, piece by piece, and places St. Edward in the national spotlight.

"To remember when I played here, where St. Ed's was and where it is now is mind-blowing to me," Coach Flannery said. "To be at a national stage and to be able to do what I am able to do and represent St. Ed's is something special. I was an assistant coach on this (USA Basketball) team and I haven't been an assistant coach for a long time. This taught me a lot about how much I need to depend upon my assistants and what my assistants are thinking. It gave me a different perspective of the game in working with the players, and looking at the game from the bench, and not having the pressure of being the head coach. I am learning from the coach from Mexico, the coach from Argentina, and the coach from Uruguay. Most of it is X's and O's, but I can also learn some philosophy and strategy."

This USA experience parlayed with the success of the St. Ed's basketball program has given Eric Flannery a name around basketball in general. The combination has helped him build credibility with college recruiters.

"If someone wants to get credibility with college coaches, he has to be honest with them about his evaluation. We're not always right. Obviously I love these kids like they are my own. I'm going to brag about them and think they are a little bit better than what they are; but I think through my honesty, they'll at least take a look and judge for themselves. They take a look at the players and then they do their own evaluation. The work I do at USA basketball has helped that out a lot, too. They know I have seen the best players in the country so I have something to compare them to. I know what the good players look like and how they play. I can judge my own players based on that."

Outside of St. Ed's, Coach Flannery serves on the coaching staff of the USA Under-16 team that won the gold medal in the FIBA Americas Championship in Uruguay in 2013 and the U-17 team that won the gold in the World Championships in Dubai in 2014. The USA U-16 team qualified for the World Games the following year as a U-17 team.

He coached LeBron James with USA Basketball in the early '00s and was the head coach of one of the McDonald's All-American teams in 2010 in Columbus.

"That was quite an honor to coach in that McDonald's All-American game," Coach Flannery said. "Usually they have someone 65 years old at the end of his career coaching those games. I was able to do it at a young age (38). It was an honor I was able to enjoy because of my success at St. Ed's. I've been fortunate enough to get the recognition from coaching in the McDonald's game and the two gold-medal teams. A lot of coaches would like to do that."

His brother Jim was an assistant to him on the McDonald's team.

Just as those traveling for athletic diplomacy around the world are worthy of the USA jersey, the national spotlight on St. Edward basketball has made it more vital for those student-athletes such as the ones on the 2013-14 championship team to be worthy of the jersey.

Chapter 14

Being Worthy of the "Family"

One of the things that could be extracted from the student-athletes' written Jersey exercise (Chapter Two) is that they see themselves as part of the St. Ed's "family," something that will stay with them forever. They are members of the general St. Edward family as well as the St. Ed's basketball family.

Coach Flannery tries to create a family atmosphere and selects his coaches based on how well they fit into the family structure. He picks his players the same way. It is no coincidence that there were two cousins, Sean Flannery and Jack Flannery, the sons of coaches Eric and Jim respectively, on the most recent state championship team. Both state championship teams had a nephew of Coach Flannery on them. In 1998, it was Tim Smith. Still there is no nepotism. Flannery has cut other nephews.

It was fitting that Sean Flannery's first career assist as a varsity player in 2013-14 was to his cousin Jack.

"I mean it when I say that with staff, coaches and just people in general, I try to seek out people I can trust," Coach Flannery said. "It goes a long way. The kids who are around the program see how the coaches get along and treat one another and trust one another. I don't care a lot about my staff X's and O's wise. I care about guys I can trust who are going to be good to the kids and good to me and represent the school."

Considering his brother Jim is on staff, trust within families plays into it. The Gallaghers, Danny and T.J., are both on staff, and their father, Franny Gallagher, coached Eric Flannery when the latter was in high school. Dan Gallagher is a varsity assistant, T.J. is the head freshman Green coach and his dad assists him with the team.

"Those are people whom I have known for a long, long time and have been around," Coach Flannery said. "To have their family together, it shows the players that here's an entire family on staff."

With the Gallaghers, it started with Dan Gallagher being offered the head freshman coaching job. He had that job for about four years and then T.J. graduated from St. Ed's and went to Tri-C Westlake. Coach Flannery hired him to help coach one of the freshman teams (St. Ed's has two freshman teams, one called the Gold and the other the Green). T.J. Gallagher was the assistant coach for Coach Josh Nugent on the Green team.

"My brother was the head Gold team coach; we didn't actually coach together," T.J. said. "We were actually on the opposite ends. When Josh Nugent moved up to head JV coach, I was moved up to head freshman coach and that was when I brought on my dad to be an assistant with me. Having the whole family in the fold helped a ton especially when I was starting. Growing up, I was watching him and my dad coach. My dad coached me while I was at OLA (Our Lady of Angels) in grade school. My brother was the assistant coach. Just coming in and getting my first coaching job ever as an assistant at St. Ed's, I found it good to always have my brother there to help me out."

It also helps that T.J. and Danny Gallagher are roommates.

"We talk about basketball all the time," T.J. said. "We have never made it a rivalry. We always supported each other whether we won or lost."

Then there are Josh Nugent and his brother Devin Nugent. Josh is the head JV coach and Devin is the scorekeeper for both the varsity and JV teams as well as for football at St. Ed's.

"I have known the Nugents almost their entire lives," Coach Flannery said. "We are doing this together with people that we trust. When things go bad, because they will at some time, we have to have people we can trust, people I can go down together with. Winning a state championship becomes that much more enjoyable. Having my son and nephew on the team was special. Having my brother with me was special."

While Josh Nugent was on staff three years ago, Devin was looking for a job at the time. He needed some extra money and was looking for an opportunity. It came as a result of Coach Flannery acting as an Edsman of good service.

"Devin has been doing great for three years as varsity scorekeeper," said Josh Nugent. "Jack Sheridan was stepping down as the scorer. Flan asked, 'Do you know anyone who wants to do it?' I said Devin. I get a thrill watching Devin interact with the players. I had no idea it was going to evolve into the kind of respect he has for the players, and the coaches. I used to baby sit Sean and P.J. when Coach Flan lived down the street. We speak about it and how every coach talks about team, team, team. He talks about family. One can go to other programs and they'll talk about the family atmosphere, but he's got guys who baby sat his kids who are coaching for him now. He brings in brothers of coaches and he has his own brothers and nephews on staff. When we talk to people who leave here, whether it is a player who has left here or a coach who has moved on, they'll come back and talk about how fondly they remember what it was like here. I'm incredibly grateful to be a part of it and excited that I get to share moments like that with my brother. The Gallagher family is great."

The rest of the staff are "St. Ed's family" guys, people such as James Crawford who played for Flannery and returned. Then there is Pete Campbell who coached at St. Ed's when Flannery first started coaching. He also is a St. Edward grad. "I've known him for the last 25 years," Flannery said. "We went to high school around the same time."

Coaches have to act in a family-like manner, prompting the players on the team to come together as a family.

"I have to practice what I preach," Coach Flannery said. "If I talk about family and then don't have anything to show them, I'd be a hypocrite. I'm not just talking about the coaches. I'm talking about my wife being around and my kids being around. All these guys in the program know who they are. My wife does a tremendous job of allowing these players to be a part of our family when they need to be."

While he has allowed players to feel as though they are a part of his own family as well as the St. Ed's family, Coach Flannery also has non-basketball playing blood family members, who are also part of the St. Ed's family.

Flannery's nephew, Mike O'Malley, who now wrestles and plays football at St. Edward, played grade-school basketball and also wrestled in his pre St. Ed's days.

"He did play basketball; I coached him with AAU," Coach Flannery said. "He knew he was leaning toward wrestling so he did that."

Pat Flannery, the son of Dr. Flannery, was a hockey player and not a wrestler. Joe Flannery before him was a wrestler.

"Granted, I cut a couple (nephews) who were freshmen, but I cut them when they were freshmen and they just chose not to come out after that," Coach Flannery said. "I don't think I ever cut a nephew who was trying out for varsity."

Jim had three who went to St. Ed's. Dr. Flannery, the second oldest, had two at St. Ed's. His sister Kelly had three. His sister Michelle had one. His sister Judi O'Malley currently has two boys in the school and has six boys altogether. His sister Mary Lou did not have children attending St. Edward, but has two boys. The oldest is going to Lakewood and is the first nephew not to come to St. Edward. He and his brother are soccer players. Their dad is a soccer coach at Lakewood, and they wanted to play for their dad. Coach Flannery's brother Bryan hasn't had any boys at St. Edward yet, but he has a son and he'll end up coming to St. Ed's.

Along with a family atmosphere among the coaches and players, at St. Ed's there is also a family atmosphere among the coaches themselves.

Coaching is taken very seriously at St. Ed's because student-athletics is taken very seriously. For all sports, St. Ed's has 110 assistant and head coaches. Counting part-time and volunteer coaches, the basketball program has more than a dozen on staff. Some might think that is too many; but in the way that player number 18 is as important as player number one, each coach brings something unique to the program and is responsible for some of the success Coach Flannery has experienced.

"We don't have a big staff just to intimidate other teams," Coach

Flannery said. "With maturation for a basketball coach or any coach at any level comes the ability to learn to delegate. It's learning to trust and knowing my ego is not that big that I have to control everything. When I first started coaching, I coached everything. I wanted to control everything."

As in any job, that can simply wear someone out. The top attributes of assistant coaches are trust and responsibility.

"I have to give them responsibility or they will tune me out," Coach Flannery said. "One assistant would just work with the big guys. Another coach would have the responsibility to work with the guards. When I didn't have to, it gave me time to walk away and watch. I could see the bigger picture. Then I allowed guys to call plays. Having, a special-teams coach who can work on all the inbounds plays allows me not to worry about it. I can oversee things and tell them things I don't like."

He can correct things that others do. It has saved him time and has allowed him to pay more attention to his thoughts. St. Ed's has a bigger staff than when he first started, and each is assigned something. Flannery's growth has come in his allowing people to voice their opinions and keeping them involved.

Coaches appreciate being able to take over some of the work and to have a say in how to execute the plan, but they also buy into Coach Flannery's philosophy the same way the players do: that everything has to be earned, that each player and coach counts for the same as any other, and that it is important to be close as a team/family.

"When the players and coaches are taking ownership, it starts at the top," said Ansberry, the former inbounds coach and still a teacher at St. Ed's. "Flan does a good job when we would be sitting in the office after practice to talk and he would do a great job of delegating. He's good at knowing and getting a feel for his players, but also at trusting his assistants. I remember my last play here and I remember Ryan Angers had the ball and got open and missed the shot, but Matt Stainbrook tipped it in to send it into overtime. I was excited, but selfishly I was nervous because that was the play I drew up. Then I snapped myself out of it – this is a team thing. Then I think, 'I can't believe Flan trusted me to call that play.'

"We could have a dictator type coach who does not delegate and has his hands on everything. Ultimately he is going to make the final decisions, but to give his assistants more say is amazing. I have two assistants at Lake Ridge. I trust them, but sometimes they are saying things I don't agree with right away. How does one deal with that? Flan would give great advice. He'd say, 'Let the guy talk and then talk to him afterword. If he is saying something that is wrong, then just jump in and say it. Let them know you are in charge.'"

If a coach wants to move on and get a better situation elsewhere, Coach Flannery is supportive of it because it grows the St. Ed's coaching tree.

"He was always asking, 'Brian, what are your goals?' and I would tell him, 'I want to coach here and be a head coach somewhere and eventually get down to Columbus,'" Ansberry said. "'I love the school. I would never leave here unless there were a great opportunity.' Flan always said, 'I'll help you get any job you can. I would never want you to leave here and take an assistant job somewhere else, but if you have a head coaching job, go.'"

Before leaving for Lake Ridge, Coach Ansberry talked to Coach Flannery about a number of jobs that were open. When the job from Lake Ridge was offered to him, they sat down and figured it out. They talked about the pros and cons. His uncles had played at St. Ed's in the 1960s. His dad (Jay Ansberry) works in the Development Office with the alumni. He grew up in a family of four boys and one girl. All four boys went to St. Ed's. His uncle, Walt Violand, who had just passed away, played on some good St. Ed's teams in the 1960s and went to Providence to play basketball. Violand was the first one from St. Ed's to get a major scholarship. Ansberry learned what he needed to learn at St. Ed's and moved on to be a head coach.

"I give them (assistant coaches) advice outside of coaching X's and O's" Coach Flannery said. "They'll come back and we'll talk about it. My advice is more along the lines of how someone handles himself and whether he is OK with what he is doing. Most of the advice is how to handle parents, student-athletes, and situations. The longer someone is here the more opportunity I have had with guys who do that – to come back and talk."

Even though St. Ed's has a lot of assistant coaches, they don't just sit around and twiddle their thumbs. They all have a purpose.

"There is an outside perception that 'wow, they have so many guys,'" Coach Nugent said. "Just like the roles of the players, Coach Flan is good at letting us know what our roles are and when. JV and freshman coaches go out to the other sites (during the playoffs). We're always thinking one step beyond. Coach Flan doesn't scout and he shouldn't. He's the head coach and should be thinking about whom he has in front of him for that game. His immediate assistants are thinking for the next game. Coaches (Pete) Campbell, (Jason) Bratton, (Joe) Scarpitti and I are going out to Midview while we are still playing in Brecksville."

A number of former St. Ed's players, such as Ansberry, have come back to coach at St. Ed's, but one doesn't necessarily have to have been a player in order to be a coach for Coach Flannery and to remain a part of the "family." Sometimes he sees things in people that would make them great coaches regardless of their playing experience. Such was the case for Danny Gallagher, T.J. Gallagher and Josh Nugent. All three were team managers before becoming St. Ed's coaches.

"I'm not sure it's me," Coach Flannery said about his managers turned coaches. "A lot of that just goes along with the program itself because we have had a lot of success, and now we have kids at the school who realize they can't play any more or maybe they never really wanted to play, but just wanted be a part of it. They started learning about the game and really loved what they were doing. My thing was always simply to encourage. Someone doesn't need to be a great player to be a part of the team and stay involved. I encourage them to simply put in the time as much as anyone else in the game. Sitting on the bench and listening to coaches and watching teams play is what coaches do. They are already starting to coach and getting into that mindset."

Coach Flannery has helped managers become college managers. They start as managers at St. Ed's, become managers in college, and some then become coaches. If this is what they want to continue to do, he'll call their colleges and talk to their coaches.

"I know those guys are looking for good managers and good people who are recommended," Coach Flannery said. "It's been a little uncanny how many we have had."

Conor Donelon, who was a manager at St. Ed's, became a manager in college and is now a college assistant coach. Pete Kahler (director of basketball operations at the University of Michigan) played for Flannery. He was going to play in college but instead became a college manager and is now an assistant coach. Jack Hayes, a manager at Xavier, had been a manager at St. Ed's. Then there are Nugent and the two Gallaghers.

"I don't know what it is," Coach Flannery said. "Maybe it's just the fact that I made them feel welcome and a part of it. They were part of the basketball family. They weren't players or great players."

The former manager turned-coach, Nugent now gets students coming to him wanting to be managers.

"Having done it and the fact that I have had managers, I have come to realize they are the most important people that we have," Nugent said. "We don't just say that. Coach Flan allowed me to go out and scout games. He asked for my advice from time to time (while he was a manager). I was talking in front of the team and I was a senior manager."

One day Nugent was leaving his car at a mutual friend's graduation party when he was 20 years old and Coach Flannery asked if he was still interested in coaching. He started helping out with the freshmen while he was still at college. He has been doing it for eight years now. He was on campus at John Carroll his first two years of college but moved back home and commuted just so that he could start his coaching career. He went to school during the day and worked his schedule so that he could be at the gym at 3 o'clock every day. Some days he had to go back to school after practice, but obviously it was worth it for him. Remembering how it was for him in college, Coach Flannery was merely acting under the Holy Cross philosophy, paying it forward.

Nugent's first six years were with the freshman team – two years as an assistant coach under Ansberry (the head freshman coach at the time) and four years as the head freshman coach. During his last year as a freshman coach, he had the group who would be seniors in 2014-15, a group that went undefeated as a freshman team and lost only two games as a JV team. Some of them were part of the state championship team as juniors.

Others have returned to help out for a summer or for parts of a season.

Former players who have been worthy of the jersey have remained part of the St. Ed's basketball "family."

Pete Latkovic, who was on the '98 team, came back and coached for a few years. He took a job with Spalding because of his basketball connections at St. Ed's and currently assists Ansberry at Lake Ridge. Sam Clancy from the '98 team still plays pro basketball outside the country; but in the summers when he comes home, he still works out at St. Edward. He just keeps the St. Ed's family informed as to how he is doing. His brother, Samario, is now coaching college basketball at Alderson Broaddus. He came back and helped out over the summer. Donelon is the assistant coach for former Cleveland State coach Rollie Massimino at Northwood in Florida. Donelan was Flannery's primary manager. Mark Murray, who graduated a couple years ago, went to Capital, opted out and now he is helping as a video coordinator for the women's basketball team at Ohio State. Then there is Steve Logan, player on the championship team of '98 and aid to the championship team of '14 as orchestrator of the great point guard development project. Logan went to Cincinnati, was an All-American, and was drafted in the NBA. Logan once outscored a team in college by himself. He's in the University of Cincinnati Hall of Fame for basketball. Logan works particularly with the point guards, but also helps Jim Flannery with the other guards.

T.J. Gallagher has been instrumental in getting the players in shape physically. T.J. learned a lot about conditioning and working out from being the equipment manager for football and working alongside the strength coaches.

"I have had people say to me, 'Your guys just look like men," Coach Flannery said. "'The way those guys look on the floor, they look bigger and stronger. What did they do and what did you do?' The answer is T.J. and what he did with their strength and conditioning. We do agility every Monday. We work out two days a week. During the offseason, we start at 7 a.m. The dedication is not only what the kids had but what T.J. had."

That's why the staff has grown throughout the years.

Danny Gallagher is his out-of bounds-coach or special-teams coach, a responsibility Ansberry used to handle. He calls the play when the Eagles have an inbound situation. Danny G. is in charge of the CYO program, the youth basketball program (Cleveland Old School Athletics), and the AAU component of it.

Delvon Blanton, who is Delvon Roe's dad, came on staff after Delvon graduated in a desire to give back to a school that had given so much to his son. Blanton is the individual workout coach. He works with student-athletes on individual skill development and fundamentals. If someone needed to develop within an hour's time, Coach Delvon would have him working his tail off for a straight hour without hesitation, improving that player's game. After practice he works on drills and with the big guys.

"When my son was at St. Ed's I did not want to step on Coach Flan's toes and get the negativity of people possibly saying he's on the staff only because his son's on the team," Coach Blanton said. "I always followed Coach Flan even before my son got there. I liked everything he did in terms of the discipline and education and basketball. I coached LeBron's AAU teams. I wanted to bring in kids who had the similar background that my son had. The guys have to understand something. When someone can reach out and go to a school like St. Ed's, he gains so much more than what he could in his own home community. If he wants to be diverse and go to a place where he has to be responsible for things in every day life, he'll go somewhere like St. Ed's.

"If he's not doing right in life and with his grades, he is not going to play. St. Ed's gives discipline and competition every day. Whatever someone learns in life, he's going to have to learn character first and take care of one's responsibilities. We have a thing called collective responsibility. We're all in the same circle. When one person does something wrong, we are all accountable for it. When my son went to St. Ed's, I watched the good and I watched the bad. When he got injured, that caused a lot of heartache because there was unfinished business. This year it felt so special not just for him but for Lakewood, the kids, the community. Other times they came so close, but they didn't finish because of certain things. In life, things happen. When they do, we have to continue and keep fighting (next play, learning from losses, etc.)."

Tom Bodle is the statistics overseer and director of basketball operations. Bodle also took over the freshman Gold team (T.J. is the freshman Green coach) in 2013, so he had been head freshman coach.

"I am blessed in the sense that I have a number of assistants," Coach Flannery said. "People want to come and help. Former players come back and want to be a part of it; I am very bad at saying no to people like that. People want to sacrifice their time and want to help me, so it is hard to say no to those types of people."

Along with Bodle, Nugent and Jason Bratten, who are JV coaches, are in the building every day so they are on top of things. They help if players are struggling.

"They want to be in my ear, but they know when to talk to me and when not to," Coach Flannery said. "If I get mad at them throughout the season, there is never any second guessing or questioning – it's always what could I do to help? They might tell me when they think I am wrong, which is fine because we have such good relationships. I might tell them to go pound salt, but we have that great relationship.

"All I care about is loyalty. I have only guys on my staff I can trust. If someone wants to be on my staff it is his job to be trustworthy and that might take some time. I know they are not walking out of here saying bad things. They are all good people and they want to be here."

Coach Flannery cares more about whether he can trust someone, how loyal and how hard he works. Is an assistant comfortable enough to tell Flannery when he is wrong?

"That's what I want," he explained. "Is he going to be a yes man and sit there and agree with everything I say? If one looks at our staff, he sees guys who want to come back every year. We don't lose guys. We lost Brian last year because he went to a head job. If you want to be a head coach, don't wait for me. During the tough times they stuck with us. They have the attitude, 'We'll be with you when it gets good again.' That shows up for the players too. If there is a disruptive coach or there is one that is not loyal, players see through that. That hurts a team. Ultimately everything falls on me because I am the head coach, but I don't think I am any better than any of these guys."

So in order to be worthy of the jersey, one has to buy into the family concept, learning from their coaches, the coaches' families, their own families, and all the way up to the head coach.

Chapter 15

Worthy of Staying or Leaving

Through the past two decades, Coach Eric Flannery has become a fixture at St. Edward. When people think of St. Edward basketball, they at the same time think of Coach Flannery. With the success he has had, outside observers might assume that he would never want to leave. Conversely, if he has had so much success, it is a wonder to some why he has not already moved on to college coaching. Although he had success early and for the most part it has continued, it wasn't always that way for Coach Flannery as there were times that he had inklings of moving on from St. Ed's. Many are glad he didn't.

When someone starts his career by going to a final four three years in a row, he expects things. The following three years after the three final fours St. Ed's had a great player in Jawad Williams. By everyone's definition, he was a very good high school basketball player. Williams was heavily recruited by Matt Doherty, who was at Notre Dame at the time. When Doherty attained the head job at North Carolina, Williams followed him to play for the Tar Heels. They had high expectations because they had a good player. Flannery was later to learn it was not enough to just have a good player. Eventually this became the foundation of a player earning one's spot, buying into the program and bonding.

"We didn't necessarily have a good team during those three years," Coach Flannery said. "We had particular players who, in my opinion, thought they were very good but weren't. Along with that came some parents with issues. After winning a state championship, the expectations are high so the parents get higher expectations. That was true at St. Ed's. We encountered things from alumni and boosters and that was on me."

This meant that Coach Flannery had the notion that maybe St. Ed's was not the place for him. A sub-.500 year followed by two more years of failing to get out of the district hardly matched having gone to the final four three times and winning a state championship.

"I was questioning myself," Coach Flannery said. "We win a state championship and then we have to rebuild and do it all over again. While we were not seeing much success and experiencing some losses, I was having some unhappiness. I wasn't happy with the kids that I had at the time. I wasn't happy with me and the way I coached. I wasn't happy with the results. I questioned myself: am I a good coach and is this the right place for me? Should I look now and try to make some money and go to a public school? I thought maybe I could get into a less pressured situation and find a better arrangement for my family. I wasn't happy, but a lot of it was on me. A lot of it was the way I coached and maybe I wasn't doing things the right way."

At that time he thought about changing the way he approached the players and parents, doing things differently and doing them for the right reasons.

"If I am going to lose, I am going to lose my way," Coach Flannery said. "If my way doesn't work, I can at least look at myself in the mirror and know that I am working hard and doing it the way I want to do it. If the administration or boosters don't like that, then this isn't going to be the place for me."

He interviewed at nearby Avon High School and Rocky River High School. Through the interviewing process, he wound up in the final two at both places, but in both scenarios he pulled his name. He never was offered a job officially and never turned down a job officially.

"At both points I thought I was rushing into it. Really something was pulling me back," Coach Flannery said. "Something was making me say, 'I need to stay here at St. Ed's.' It was just my way of reaching out and seeing what was out there, but I never felt comfortable leaving. In the end, it came down to more of a gut feeling of 'this is where I belong.' It might not have been necessarily the best choice for me financially or for my family, but it always seemed to be the right choice."

During these years, 2000 and 2001, he might have questioned if St. Ed's was where he wanted to be, but at that point he had made that decision that he was going to do things his way. Some people thought he was too laid back as a head coach or he didn't attract the right players. He had people telling him how he should be coaching, which led him to question himself.

"I am going to coach the way I want to coach X's and O's," Coach Flannery reflected on the times. "I am a defensive-minded person, but I am going to adjust to my players. I want young people to come to St. Ed's because they want to be here at St. Ed's, that they want to get a great education and they want to get the Holy Cross spiritual component."

He decided he was not going to offer potential student-athletes anything. When a coach is young and new he tries to convince people to come and play. After 2001 he said forget it. He wanted student-athletes who were going to be at St. Ed's for the right reasons.

"I'm not going to try to talk anybody into playing basketball at St. Ed's," Coach Flannery explained. "I will talk about our program and our school, but I want them to make the decisions themselves. Since then I think we have lost some talented players because some eighth graders wanted to hear they are going to start or play varsity. I refuse to promise anything. Since then, we have gotten students, families, and parents who want to be here. They are here for the right reasons. They want to come here because they know they are going to be pushed academically. They know they are in a good community, and they know they are going to be coached in the right way."

With that, if they play, they know they have earned their playing time. From that point on, nobody at St. Ed's was promising them anything. Over the last 10 or 12 years it has been a better experience for him. He was winning or losing with great student-athletes who wanted to be at the school and great families that wanted to be supportive, but there were exceptions. After those two public school interviews he started doing it his way and became comfortable with the way he coached.

"I might lose a lot of games in a year and I might be disappointed because I want to win, but I will be OK because I am doing it the way I want to do it," he explained. "That really was a crossroads I had back in 2001. It had something to do with losing, but it had a lot to do with 'am I doing this for the right reasons? Am I listening to too many people?' At that point I developed tough skin. I can now very easily turn off any criticism, any discouraging words. It still hurts, but I have no problem dealing with it. I am able to put it all in perspective, and I think that started in 2001 when I just said that no matter what I do, people are going to say something whether good, bad or indifferent. Once I realized that, this job became easy."

While exploring the Avon and Rocky River jobs, there was some testing of the waters, but he didn't pull his name out of the pool for fear of having to make a decision.

"The Avon situation seemed to be more of a testing the waters," Coach Flannery recalled. "The Rocky River job was a little closer to home and I thought it was a very good teaching and coaching situation. I was down to the final two and my son, P.J., (a freshman at St. Ed's starting in 2014) was born. I was supposed to go into my final interview. I called and said I know I am supposed to have my interview today, but my wife is going into labor and I am going to pull out my name and said, 'Give it to the other person.'"

He has had some colleges, mostly Division III, that had asked him if he would be interested in their head coaching jobs. He has turned all of them down without even going through the process. He also has had some public schools contact him to see if he would be interested in their positions. He has yet to say yes or take any of them seriously.

In one other situation recently he was approached about a job. In the summer of 2013 he was being considered for the head coaching position of the Canton Charge, the Cleveland Cavaliers' team in the NBA's developmental league.

"They actually had called me to ask about another person who had applied for the job who coached on an international team," he explained. "They thought that with my ties with USA basketball, I might know the person. In that same conversation it was said, 'Would you be interested in this job?' I said, 'I would talk to you about it. We need to sit down.'"

They arranged a lunch meeting with three Cavs executives. They told him what the job would entail. He talked to then-coach Mike Brown about it.

"When I get into those situations, I have to weigh the good and the bad," he said. "We had to think about the future. Mike's thing was that this was a good way to get into the NBA. 'In a year or two I could interview you for an assistant coach job with the Cavs,' Mike said. Mike and I have had a good relationship. They said Mike is the most stable guy in the organization right now because he just signed a five-year contract." (Brown was let go for a second time by the Cavs in the spring of 2014)

In that conversation there was nothing official in writing, but they offered him the job if he wanted it. He went home and talked it over with Lori. Being the D League, it wasn't a huge salary and they probably would have liked for him to move to Canton. He would have been spending a lot of time with the Cavs as well as serving as coach of the NBDL league team.

"It came down to this. Here are my boys who have been waiting their whole lives to come to St. Ed's and possibly play for me," Coach Flannery said. "That opportunity is just presenting itself at the time with Sean being a sophomore and P.J. coming in as a freshman. I thought the timing was bad. Had that offer come to me five years ago or even five years from now, I might consider it. I simply called them back and told them thank you very much for the opportunity and offer, but I am going to pass. I count my blessings that I did pass it up."

He would not have experienced a state championship again and wouldn't have shared it with his son, which was special. Also, with Brown being released in the spring of 2014, he might have been in limbo with the job as of the 2014-15 season. By putting all things together, it was another good decision to staying put.

"I have to go with my heart and following with what I think is the right thing for me and not necessarily following the money and following the prestige of being an NBA coach at some point down the line," Coach Flannery said.

Avon and River would have been a short drive from home. Although he has reached national recognition with the St. Ed's program and with USA Basketball, Coach Flannery does not care to stray much from his origin. While the job he has now was his dream job when he was young, he would still consider another "dream" job.

"This is home; even to this day I don't necessarily see myself doing anything else," Coach Flannery said. "It doesn't mean that at some point I might not get the itch to try something new. I've always said if I wanted to coach in college, it would be at a place like Cleveland State (his other alma mater). I could build a Division I program right here in the city of Cleveland."

As far as jobs go, Coach Flannery is happy with the decisions he has made, but more importantly he learned something from both high school opportunities as well as the D League situation. He doesn't second guess his decisions.

"I think about the what-ifs, but it is a good lesson," Coach Flannery said. "People say the grass isn't always greener on the other side and that couldn't be truer for me. I have had tough times here, but it has been an unbelievable journey. This is what I love to do and I am doing it. The relationships I have built, the people I have met, the kids I have coached, the doors that have opened for me with USA Basketball are great."

It has been the case that many a coach leaves his coaching position once his biological children have graduated. St. Ed's has a situation that is the antithesis of that with Delvon Blanton returning to coach after his son, Delvon Roe, had graduated. During the championship season and over the next four years, Coach Flannery has or will have coached his two sons. People want to spend time with their children and someone who is a coach probably wants to coach his own child. If the child goes on to college, the parent may want to follow him. Sometimes he will give up the position to do that.

"I don't plan on leaving; if I did, it would have been before they were born," Coach Flannery said. "I've done it since they've been growing up. I mean this, I consider all the players who have played for me to be some part of my family. I have that connection. It won't be that once my two sons are gone that I lose the connection with everybody else. I still have that family connection, that family feeling."

His experiences in the early '00s including an overachieving team in 2002 that achieved by doing things his way (earning, buying in, bonding, etc.), Flannery has realized that for good things to come, it often takes time.

"It's hard to build tradition and relationships," Coach Flannery said. "A lot of things we want to do to build a program we can't do within just a couple years. We have what we have because of longevity. I've had the good and bad times. Administrations and parents get tired of people quitting if they don't have instant succcss or they aren't taking care of their child. It is about our society. People want things done now and they want it done for them. I have been fortunate to be at a place like St. Ed's, where winning is important and still be the head coach after 18 years."

Coaching longevity comes from earning the worthiness to don a jersey early on, which is what Coach Flan did back in the 1980s as a student-athlete.

Chapter 16

Power Shift

One annual meeting that is almost as intense as the St. Ed's-St. Ignatius rivalry is that between St. Edward and St. Joseph (VASJ). This rivalry started as a great football battle. St. Joseph, an all-boys Division I school that opened shortly after World War II during the Truman years just like St. Ed's, became a coed school (renamed Villa Angela-St. Joseph) in the early 1990s. Since then it has won five state championships in basketball in three different divisions.

In football, the Eagles and Vikings had many great games including the former Charity Game, played at Cleveland Municipal Stadium. Those along the lake shore looked forward to the St. Ed's-St. Joe's football game as one that was certain to be intense. VASJ has also been involved in football state tournaments (The Vikings won the football state championship in Division II in 1989 as St. Joe's). St. Joe's and St. Ed's were known as mainly football schools through the 1960s and 1970s. It wasn't until around the late 1970s with the arrival of Clark Kellogg that St. Joe's started to become known as a basketball school. Kellogg still holds the record for most points scored in a state championship game with 51 in 1979, yet the first state championship at the school would not arrive until 12 years later.

Still, St. Joe's had arrived as a "basketball" school while St. Ed's was still considered a "football" school and the No. 1 winter sport in terms of success was wrestling.

St. Edward's director of basketball operations during the 2013-14 championship season as well as head freshman Gold coach and assistant varsity coach, Tom Bodle was an assistant coach and athletic director at VASJ for some of those state championships. In many ways the Vikings' situation was similar to St. Edward's in that they did it through the great bonding of players instead of relying on one star like a Kellogg or Treg Lee in the years they did not win state titles.

"Good teams have that player who does not get playing time," Coach Bodle explained. "At St. Joe's we had a team in 1994 that won the state championship in Division II, and we had an all-star player named Mel Levett. We had a student-athlete from the soccer team who was a back-up point guard and my point guard when I was the freshman coach. He didn't get a lot of playing time. He was like the 13th guy. He got time during garbage situations. He worked harder than anyone in practice.

"Our point guard was Babe Kwasniak, Ted's son (former VASJ Coach Ted Kwasniak). When we asked them to write who his hero was, Babe wrote that it was Gary Wilson because 'he made me work harder than anyone in my life.' He played well in practice. We had a good group of practice players that made the starters work hard. One player was hurt most of the year, but he came to every practice. He didn't have to. He was a football student-athlete and wound up receiving a football scholarship. This group of seniors (St. Ed's in 2014) reminded me of that year. They were tight knit, worked hard and didn't complain. Whenever that player would get in the game that year, the crowd would get into it. It was like when we got Pisco or Flannery or the bench mob into the game. Good teams that are successful have those types of kids."

St. Joe's and VASJ dominated the basketball series between St. Joe's and St. Ed's from the 1950s to the 1990s. They stopped playing in football in the 1990s because VASJ was shrinking in enrollment rapidly. In basketball, however, even after VASJ went from D-I and then to D-II and then to D-III and then to D-IV it still played a D-I type of schedule, which included St. Ed's.

During the Flannery years, St. Ed's has dominated the St. Ed's-VASJ series. St. Ed's has gone 16-2, including winning the last 14 straight.

"They were dominant and moved divisions and now we have been winning," said Flannery as he knocked on wood. "It says a lot about our program and who we are. Yes, they can talk about divisions, but as far as the private schools go, there is not a whole lot that separates them in basketball. Because of St. Joseph's history, it will always be a powerhouse in basketball. I can't explain it (the Eagles' record against VASJ under Flannery). To beat them, I thought we had to play really well. I thought they were as good as or better than us. It could be luck.

"Everyone wants to talk about Ed's-Ignatius. It is our rival, but when we talk about the landscape of basketball in northeast Ohio, part of me likes to think that we have taken that over as the team to beat -- what St. Joe's was in the '70s and '80s. St. Joe's is still highly regarded and well respected. The record speaks for itself. St. Joe's is right there with Ignatius as far as basketball goes."

Some of the success Coach Bodle had at VASJ rubbed off on the coaches and student-athletes at St. Ed's and could be part of the reason the team was able to win the state championship in 2014.

"When he first came over here, I don't think he had a whole lot of intention to coach," Coach Flannery said. "He came here because he secured a teaching job. I approached him simply because I knew him as being on the St. Joe's staff. Here's a guy who has had a lot of success and should know what he is doing. He was part of a winning culture. Having him here as a teacher is even better because he is in the school. His experience at St. Joe's would be valuable to me. He could give us some advice and certain tidbits about how to handle certain things. To finally win a state championship with him on staff is great. He wasn't around for the first one."

Coach Bodle's combined experience with state championship teams at two schools makes him a rather unique person.

"Tom Bodle has been around a long time and I mean that respectfully," Coach Flannery said. "Tom is valuable behind the scenes, but he is also knowledgeable. When I need clarification on something we are doing, and he may not know this, I go to him and ask and listen to what he says because of his knowledge and experience."

With an experience that goes way back to the 1960s, Coach Bodle has been involved in many St. Ed's-St. Joe's epic battles.

"They (the basketball teams in the '60s, '70s and '80s at St. Joe's) were good but football always took precedent," Coach Bodle said. "St. Ed's was always football. The St. Ed's-St. Joe's rivalry for football was big. For wrestling it was big. St. Joe's had good wrestling teams. In basketball, St. Joe's just dominated. Ed's was considered to have football players playing basketball. They started getting basketball types in and Eric kept that up. As many state wrestling championships we (St. Ed's) have, the excitement in the school when we have a basketball championship is always higher. It's more of a crowd sport. Even the wrestling coaches, Coach (Greg) Urbas, get really excited about the basketball team. Even though we have two state championships and 29 in wrestling, those two state championships are highly regarded."

While Villa Angela-St. Joseph won the state championship in Division IV in 2013, it was playing in Division III in 2014 and going after a state title in its fourth different division. As it unfolded toward the end, it nearly grabbed that honor. St. Ed's was going after the same honor in Division I.

While on this journey of the 2013-14 season, the Eagles would not go right from Shaker to VASJ. They had a tough Cleveland Central Catholic team to contend with in between the two games.

The Vikings were ranked in the top 10 in the state in Division III, but so was Cleveland Central Catholic, also one of the finer small-school programs in the area and still fresh from a state runner-up finish in 2011 in Division III.

In five days, the Eagles would have to play the Ironmen at home and then the Vikings in the Viking Village. Still smarting from their loss to Shaker, the Eagles wanted to prove that they were deserving of their lofty ranking. Against these two formidable programs, they would get their chance(s).

In both games, the Eagles found themselves in tough battles.

The Ironmen would lead by five at halftime, 31-26, and the Eagles would have to have sharper shooting in the second half to pull out the 68-64, come-from-behind victory.

Against Central Catholic, the Eagles brought some bad habits from the Shaker game, shooting less than 30 percent from the field in the first half. By halftime, they knew they had to learn something from the Shaker loss and the three days of practice following it.

They did just that, shooting more than 50 percent from the field in the second half. The comparison was 9-for-33 in the first half and 14-of-26 in the second half.

"We took better shots and were able to get them out of their zone," Coach Flannery said after the game.

So from the Shaker loss the Eagles learned how to push teams out of a zone and make them play straight up and force the defensive effort by the opponent.

The Eagles were sharp shooters from the charity stripe, making 17-of-23 free-throw attempts.

St. Ed's trailed the entire second quarter.

"We moved the ball better during the second half than we had the first half, making a big difference," Coach Flannery said. "If we made one extra pass in the second half, at least we made it."

The Eagles came out with an alternative starting lineup on this Seniors' Night. They started five seniors – Pisco, Flannery, Follmer, Riley and Meyer – who had yet to start a game during the season.

"One of our downfalls the last couple games had been settling for bad shots around the basket and taking open-range jump shots," Coach Flannery said after the game.

Now that the Eagles were able to get back on the winning track, it was time for another one of those St. Ed's-VASJ battles and what a game it would be.

This one took until the end to finally belong to the Eagles, who raised their record to 18-2. The lead changed hands 19 times and the score was tied 10 times. The Eagles went on to win, 82-76.

It was one of those team efforts with five student-athletes reaching double figures in scoring. With depth playing a big factor, two of those double-figure scorers came off the bench in Riley and Meyer, each scoring 10 points.

"We were able to get the ball inside and that opened up the perimeter shots for us," Riley said. "They were able to kick it back out to us, and we were able to get the open shots. Marsalis ("Sal" Hamilton) and Kipper (Nichols) did a nice job of getting the ball out to us. Will Meyer shot some nice threes. We were able to pick at their zone and get the ball to the middle. We were able to score off the transition."

The Bench Mob played a big role in the win.

"Pat Riley and Will Meyer were keys tonight," said Coach Flannery after the game.

The Eagles had struggled against Shaker's zone nine days prior to this game, but made up for it against the Vikings.

"I thought we looked great against their zone," Coach Flannery said. "They are a good team and had some people on fire all night. We wanted to make it a fast-paced game. It's hard to play against them in a half-court game."

Hamilton and Walters each had six assists. Vuyancih had five and Nichols three.

The Eagles were very excited about the win, singing in unison on the bus the entire way home.

Chapter 17

At St. Ed's, Success Breeds Success

Basketball is one of the many student-athletic programs that have had success at St. Edward. On that March day in Columbus, the title won by the Eagles marked the 54th state championship that St. Edward student-athletic teams have won over the years.

All 54 of those state team championships have come since 1978. St. Edward's athletic program has been one of the most successful high school programs in the country. Some other schools such as New Trier in Illinois and Edina in Minneapolis have won over 100 state championships, but those are coed schools and their championships go back much further than 1978.

St. Ed's championships have come in boys' sports only, and all of them have been in Division I in any given sport, the highest division (big-school) in Ohio.

This parade of success began with the wrestling program, which was taken over by the late Howard Ferguson in 1975. The season before that it had not won a single match. Ferg, as he was known, brought a winning attitude to the program and was determined to build a powerhouse. "I will have a state championship team in five years," Coach Ferguson was quoted as saying.

He lied. He actually had a state championship in *three* years. That 1978 title included, the wrestling teams have won 28 state championships in the tournament format and one state championship in the dual-meet format (which did not begin in Ohio until 2013).

Coach Ferguson passed away in October of 1989, but he left the program in good hands. Coach Greg Urbas took over and the wrestling program has continued to win state championships.

St. Ed's is one of the few schools that can claim to have three head coaches whose teams have won 10 or more state championships. Both Ferguson's teams and Coach Urbas's teams have won at least 10 state championships.

Of those 54 state championships won by the school's various teams, 40 have come in two sports – wrestling and hockey. The third highly successful coach was Bob Whidden, whose hockey teams won 10 state championships in the 1980s, '90s and the 2000s.

Coach Whidden was an old professional player, a back-up goalie to Gerry Cheevers, one of the greatest goalies of all time, for the old Cleveland Crusaders of the long-defunct World Hockey Association. He remained in Cleveland and, after about five years of coaching youth hockey, took over the St. Ed's program and built a powerhouse, starting out with many of the players he had coached in the youth ranks.

The success of the wrestling and hockey programs rubbed off on other coaches and other student-athletes. Coach Ferguson was once quoted as saying, "If you want to be successful, surround yourself with successful people." That's the culture that has been created at St. Edward. The idea is quality. Student-athletes at St. Edward bring one another up and as one participant or team gets better, the others get better as well. It's a group effort that has only built more and more success over the years.

No school in Ohio has won as many state team championships as St. Edward. The more than 100 individual state champions in wrestling is also a record. For 24 seasons in a row, at least one St. Edward alumnus reached All America status as a collegiate wrestler. Also in the last three years, St. Ed's has added a dozen track and field individual state champions.

There is also a depth of student-athletic talent running around St. Edward High School. Of the 900 students enrolled in the school, 700 participate as student-athletes in one interscholastic sport or another at the varsity, JV, or freshman levels.

If St. Edward has four teams (wrestling, hockey, indoor track, and basketball) during the winter sports season that have won at least one state championship 33 of the last 37 years, then there must be a depth of talent. There has to be. Filling out a team with students from a school after other sports have claimed quality student-athletes would require a quantity of talent, but there is something else to it. It has a lot to do with that whole concept of playing out one's role as a team player and making the team great. Normally an individual sport, wrestling has become more of a team sport due to the dedication Coach Ferguson initiated and the legacy Coach Urbas has continued over the years.

While wrestling came of age in the 1970s at St. Edward and hockey came of age in the 1980s, it really wasn't until the 1990s that basketball came of age. At most schools, basketball is the No. 1 sport in the winter; but at St. Ed's it nearly took a back seat to wrestling and hockey until that 1988-89 season when the team on which Flannery was a member won a district and made it to the regional tournament.

"This is what is great about a place like St. Ed's, since there are not too many high schools that are comparable," Coach Flannery said. "Here at St.Ed's it is OK to be successful at whatever sport anyone is doing and everyone enjoys it. Even though wrestling and hockey were doing well in the '70s and '80s and continued to do well, there is definitely that sense of pride when they win. It might put more pressure on us to be successful, but we're happy for them and excited for our community."

The wrestling and hockey success does not necessarily take away student-athletic talent from basketball but rather has aided the basketball program in becoming successful.

"I am very happy when hockey wins a state title, and are ranked No. 1 in the state," Coach Flannery said. "I'm happy when wrestling wins a state title and a national title. It generates positive energy and brings integrity to the school."

At the same time it puzzles Coach Flannery that any kind of serious basketball success did not arrive until he became a part of the program as both a student and as a coach.

"As a player I couldn't imagine going almost 40 years of all those boys, 1,000 boys at a time, and never winning a district championship," Coach Flannery said. "When we won the district in '89, it was the closest thing, I can remember, to winning a state championship. We were cutting down the nets for the first time in the history of the school."

Since then, St. Ed's basketball teams have won 13 district championships (including the year there was an interim coach and Flannery was the top assistant) and have made 13 regional appearances. They have also made eight final-four appearances.

By the 2000s one could mention basketball in the same breath with hockey and wrestling when discussing winter sports at St. Ed's.

In fact, during three winter sports seasons St. Ed's nearly pulled off what no other high school in the country has ever accomplished, which is winning state titles in three different sports during the same sports season (not the same school *year*, but the same sports *season*: winter, spring or fall). A number of schools including St. Ed's have won three state titles during the same school *year*, but there has yet to be one to win three in a *season*.

In 1998, when St. Ed's wrestling and basketball won state titles, hockey made it to the final four before falling in the semis. In 2002, when both hockey and wrestling won, basketball made it to the final four before falling in the semis. In 2008, when hockey and wrestling won, basketball lost in the state title game.

"As a coach and person, I was following and learning from coaches like Bob Whidden, an extreme and intense competitor," Coach Flannery said. "He's a legendary hockey coach and I got to know him fairly well and learned from him how to manage things. Coach Urbas is the most genuine person around here. He is a giving person. St. Ed's is his life. I am lucky to follow in the footsteps and success of their programs, to learn from them and then to win a state championship in 1998, when they were just as happy for me.

"Wrestling is just such a prominent sport at this school with a great person at the head. I'm trying to bring that to basketball, to have that same consistency and regularity as wrestling and hockey."

The school has won 11 national championships in wrestling. Basketball reached that national status when it was ranked nationally in various polls during a number of seasons in the '90s, '00s and'10s including the two state championship years and also by being invited to prominent national tournaments.

Chapter 18

St. Ed's Basketball Greatness in the '90s, '00s, '10s

Since Eric Flannery took over as the head coach, and even during his years as a freshman and JV and assistant coach, St. Edward's basketball program has been building and improving every year.

By the mid-1990s St. Edward basketball was receiving national recognition, getting invited to several national tournaments and receiving mention in the rankings.

Before Coach Flannery officially took over during the 1996-97 season, St. Ed's had gone through five head coaches in six seasons. With such instability, it is no surprise that the program failed to emerge as one of the best in the state.

Yes, there were some good teams and some good players at St. Edward during the first four and a half decades of the school, but none that could be said in the same breath as "Ohio basketball powerhouse."

There was Rod Dieringer, who scored 50 points in a game during a season when St. Ed's had multiple 100-point-plus games in the early 1970s. There were some decent teams under Bernie Yun in the mid '70s with players like Neil Sterba, and there was the 1988-89 team that became the first Cuyahoga County team to win the Lorain Admiral King District title in two decades.

However, while St. Ed's might have been knocking on the door and putting up some decent numbers during its first four and a half decades, it had never made it to the state's final four and had been to the regional only once.

Changes needed to be made if St. Edward was going to become a state power. Changing head coaches nearly every year was not the way to go. The school needed a coach that would be stable and they had found one in Coach Flannery.

In the one season as the top assistant coach, 1995-96, the Eagles won their first regional title and made their first state final-four appearance, losing to LaSalle in the semifinals, 60-54.

After Flannery took over the head coaching position in 1996-97 at age 24, St. Edward again returned to the final four with many of the same players, the Eagles made it all the way to the state semis again, losing to Zanesville, 58-54, and closing out the season at 24-2.

Then in 1997-98, again with many of the same players from the two previous seasons, the Eagles went 26-1, ending the season as state champions with a 70-61 win against St. Ignatius.

The win was significant in two ways. First, it just so happened the two rival schools are fewer than five miles apart, yet they were bracketed in a way that they came out of different regions to advance to the state championship game to play against each other. Second, Flannery, at 25, became one of the youngest head coaches in Ohio to win a state championship in the big-school (Division I) division.

That team had the likes of Sam Clancy Jr., a post player who went on to star at the University of Southern California and in professional basketball. Clancy's dad, Sam Clancy Sr., had been a basketball star at the University of Pittsburgh as well as a member of the Pan American team and later played football for the Cleveland Browns. Sam Clancy Jr. as of 2014 was still playing professional basketball abroad.

Another top player on that championship team was Steve Logan, the point guard, who went on to star at the University of Cincinnati and later was drafted by Golden State in the NBA. A collegiate All American, Logan is now in the UC Athletics Hall of Fame.

Flannery knew he would one day have a team that would win another state championship. What he didn't realize was how long it would take to come to him.

After that first state championship season, St. Ed's hit a dry spell for a period, including a sub.500 year. Things started picking up in the 2001-2002 season.

A team that maybe wasn't expected to go far in 2001-02 went all the way to the final four before losing to Brookhaven from the Columbus area, in overtime. Brookhaven went on to win the state title in a blowout.

The 2001-2002 year would be a turning point not only in the success of the program, but in how Coach Flannery's coaching philosophy would take form.

In the 13 years between 2002 and '14, the Eagles would win 10 district titles and five regional championships, make two state championship game appearances, and win a state championship.

While talent was one of the major factors in all this winning, it wasn't the only thing. The student-athletes had to buy into the system and each one had to follow through with his role to make the whole synergistic package complete.

In the years this took place the teams went far. In the years the St. Edward players didn't quite buy into as much, the Eagles did not go far.

Some in 2012-13 bought into it and some did not despite the high level of talent. The change was that *all* of the players accepted the system and embraced their roles in 2013-14.

The most talented teams at St. Ed's were in 1996-97 and 2006-07, both making it to the final four but neither winning it all.

The 2002 team proved that a successful team could be *made* and not necessarily be a winner from raw talent alone.

The 2007-08 team had many of the same players from the previous year, but by the time the season was half over was without two of its top players in Delvon Roe and Alex Sterba, both down with injuries.

Roe would later go on to be a part of the NCAA Final Four, playing for Michigan State.

While the 1995-98 group had much of the same talent as that in 2005-08, it was the 1999-2002 group that the 2011-14 group resembled – decent talent, but one that was able to win by desire and teamwork.

The previous Flannery-coached final-four teams were 2012, 2007, 2008, 2002, '97, and '98.

The 2007-08 team was loaded with eventual collegiate student-athletes. The 2002 team and 2014 team didn't have nearly that many that went on to play college sports, but they were all sound high school *team* players.

"I don't think I ever thought when we won the first state title that it was easy," Coach Flannery said. "It is what I expect."

When those expectations aren't met year after year, it places almost a burden on him. He had to ask, "Hey, when am I going to do it again?" Was the first time just a fluke because they had a talented team and great players? Would they be able to build up the team again to the point that they would win it? They had enjoyed some success and over the years he grew to appreciate it.

"It's hard to get to the state championship game and win it," Coach Flannery said. "I started realizing as a coach that maybe it is not just about winning a state championship. It's building those relationships with the kids – trying to get the most out of their team. I enjoy that I went through all those rough times, those tough years – those disappointments to finally have that feeling again of winning a championship. That appreciation of winning the state championship was much higher than it had been the first time."

Prior to the 2014 state championship team, the 2006-08 era included a group of student-athletes that were talented enough to win at least one state championship, but the title eluded them twice.

Due to *both* depth and talent, the 2006-07 unit went down in history as one of the best teams in the regular season. They had 10 student-athletes that went on to be collegiate players.

The team included Pe'Shon Howard, who went to Maryland and finished his career at Southern Cal; Zach Price, who went to Louisville; Tom Pritchard who went to Indiana; Delvon Roe attended Michigan State; Frankie Dobbs, who went to Ohio and Bryant; Justin Staples, who played football at Illinois; Kyle Hubbard who went to Pitt for football, Cleveland State for basketball, and John Carroll for both football and basketball; Connor Tillow, who went D-II at Seton Hill; Mike Hartnett, who went to John Carroll; and Matt Salay, who went to D-II at St. Leo.

"We talk about depth; it is hard to argue against that team for being the most talented team we have had here at St. Ed's," Coach Flannery said. "They were 25-0 and won a national tournament. We didn't play well that one night (against Moeller in the state semis)."

During the mid '00s, Dobbs was a three-year varsity point guard, Hubbard (a wing in '07) was a three-year varsity player, Delbert Love wound up getting a scholarship to D-I Kennesaw State, and Roe was ranked as one of the best players in the country as a junior. Tom Pritchard was under the radar.

"Not a whole lot of people knew about Tom," Coach Flannery said. "He really had a breakout year his junior season and then in his senior season he blew up the charts."

Pe'Shon Howard and his grandfather moved to Cleveland his seventh-grade year. He went to grade school at St. Stanislaus. The reason they moved to Cleveland was that they were inspired by LeBron James. Although he had intended to go to St. Vincent-St. Mary, he wound up going to St. Ed's."

"He actually had a good year in '07 as a freshman," Coach Flannery said. "He played good quality minutes for us off the bench. After his freshman year he probably would have been our starting two guard in '07-08. We're probably a month into the school year, his sophomore year, the 2007-08 season, when he didn't show up for school on Monday. That was unlike him because he never missed a day of school. Since he lived with his grandfather, his grandfather made him come to school. The kid misses one day and it was no big deal. Then on Tuesday he wasn't here again. That Tuesday morning I had a counselor from upstairs come to my office, and she asked me if I know anything about Oak Hill Academy. 'Why would they be calling for Pe'Shon's transcripts?' I said I had no idea."

Sure enough over the weekend his grandfather had decided to drive him to Oak Hill Academy in Virginia, and drop him off. Then the grandfather moved back to California. Without warning, without discussion without anything, they literally pulled out in the middle of the night and transferred schools to Oak Hill Academy.

"I remember calling Steve Smith from Oak Hill Academy and asking him what was going on," Coach Flannery said. "He said they had called and basically said they were coming. I never talked to the grandfather. I guess maybe he couldn't take care of him any more, and the best place to drop him off was Oak Hill, where he could stay, live, get an education, and play basketball."

That season began with Alex Sterba blowing out his ACL in the opening game after having rehabbed from the year before because he had blown out his knee in a game the year before that. Then Delvon Roe was complaining after a game about a knee that bothered him. He wound up having micro-fracture surgery and missing the season. The Eagles literally lost three starters for the season by the time of the second game in 2007-08, yet they still made it to the state championship game. That says a lot about the depth the team had.

As far as records go, the two state championship teams were 26-1 ('98) and 26-2 ('14). The 2006-07 unit was the only team in school history to go undefeated during the regular season (20-0). It also won a national tournament, while the '98 and 2014 state title teams did not win a national tournament.

Of the three St. Ed's teams that made it to a state championship game, the 2013-14 team was the first one that made it after not making it to the final four the previous season, making them worthy of the jersey.

Chapter 19

Less Talent but Better Results

At St. Edward, more than once have less "talented" teams gone further than teams with more raw talent simply because they bought into Coach Flannery's philosophy, and leaders were made instead of born.

"I'll tell you what, the '98 (state championship) team wasn't the most talented from top to bottom," said Ansberry, a member of the '98 team. "Of those three teams, '96-'97-'98, we always say the '97 team was a better team. In order to win a championship, everyone has to buy into his role, know who the leader is, and if he is not going to play. Just accept that and put the team before yourself. The '98 team was only seven players deep, and I was not in that rotation. We blew a ton of teams out who were nationally ranked from the beginning.

"The reason why we won that year and not in the other years is because everyone knew his role that year. The starters knew their roles. The sixth, seventh and eighth guys knew they were going to have to come in and play some. The rest knew their roles. Coach Flan's communication is always great. He'll sit a player down and say, 'This is where you are. Can you buy into it? You're going to make the team, but you are not going to play a whole lot. If you are going to bust your butt in practice to be part of this, we want you on the team.'"

By the 2001-02 season, this concept of earning one's spot, buying into the philosophy, and accepting one's role was fully embedded, but it had taken some time.

The Eagles had a few down years after that first state championship. Despite having a high major player in Jawad Williams, the Eagles suffered a sub-.500 year (the only one in Coach Flannery's career) in 1998-99 and had decent teams leading up to the 2001-02 group.

Led by Williams, in 2000 and 2001 the Eagles made it to the district finals, just barley missing going to the regional both times.

In the 2000 district championship game, they lost to Medina, which had Tony Stockman, who went to Clemson. Stockman hit a shot with fewer than 10 seconds left to beat St. Ed's.

The following year against Strongsville, the district championship game was similar. St. Ed's had the ball with under a minute to go in a tie game and was holding for the last shot. With fewer than 10 seconds left, the Eagles turned the ball over.

Strongsville scored at the buzzer to win the district championship.

"That was Jawad's senior year," Coach Flannery said. "We had a group of guys who were talented but didn't buy into what we were doing. Those were the years I was struggling with what I was doing."

By the following year, Flannery no longer cared who someone was before he came to St. Edward. He wanted student-athletes who were willing to earn their time and roles and buy into the system, and the results were favorable. He realized it was not easy to win state championships, nor was it easy to get as far as the regional.

As a coach, Flannery had started his career 50-3 after two years.

In '99, they started three sophomores, including Williams. After winning a state championship, they were starting over to return the program to those mid-90s years of success.

"I questioned myself," Coach Flannery said. "I asked, 'Am I really any good? What do I need to do to build a program and do it the right way and not just have players on the floor who think 'I'm good?' I think I turned the corner after 2001. In 2002 we had what I consider one of our least talented teams. We had a Samario Clancy, who was a great basketball player. We had Shaun Carney (later the four-year starting quarterback for the Air Force Academy), who was a great football player but was a short, stocky basketball player. We had Ryan Keenan and Jim Kilbane, who were just football-type players."

The football types were defined as role players for basketball. They had a sophomore point guard in Trent Morgan, who had transferred from Maple Heights during his freshman year. He was a skinny, 5-8, kid who was good but not elite at the time.

"We did something with a team that wasn't extremely talented," Coach Flannery said. "That was one of the first years I got into selling the team and kids on more than basketball. I was having them buy into one another. I spent as much if not more time with them off the court than on the court. We were building not only relationships but trust in one another. We were rallying around different things, kind of what we did in 2013-14. The 2002 team had probably the most memorable tournament runs we ever had in St. Ed's basketball history with the way each game played out. We were not a top-ranked team, and yet we made it to the final four."

What precipitated off the court during the offseason provided a burning incentive to Flannery, who was the interim athletic director in 2001.

"At the end of our basketball season in '01 this (lack of getting to the regional) was leading to me to wonder what I am doing," Coach Flannery said. "A couple boosters at that time came into my office and said I need to win more and attract better players. They said something along those lines, 'You better get this thing turned around and get back to winning. We haven't won a district championship in three years.'"

Coach Flannery's response to the two boosters was that they would win the district championship and beat St. Ignatius twice the next year. They told him if he could do that, he would never hear from them again.

"If that's not enough, then I don't want to be here," he told them.

They had a decent regular season, going 15-5, but splitting with St. Ignatius and being hammered during the regular season by St. John's by 28 points in one the most one-sided defeats during Coach Flannery's tenure.

Then they were ready to go into the playoffs on a quest for their first district championship in four years. They started the tournament against Avon Lake.

They were losing by seven going into the fourth quarter in the first game of the tournament. They went to a half-court trap and ended up getting some steals and winning by three, 58-55, against the Shoremen.

In the district semifinal, the Eagles defeated Elyria handily, 70-57. The Eagles were winning the whole game. It was probably the only easy game they had in the tournament.

Next up for the district championship was Lakewood, who had beaten St. Ed's during the regular season. The Rangers had one of their best teams in history with the Fannin brothers, Matt and Mark, who later played at Navy. They had three D-I college basketball players. Samario Clancy hit a shot at the buzzer for a 62-60 St. Ed's win in double overtime.

"We could have very easily lost in the districts," Coach Flannery said, "but we won our district championship."

Coach Flannery had fulfilled one promise of winning the district championship, but the other one was still hanging in the wind. The Eagles did not beat Ignatius twice during the regular season, but would get another chance to score that second win, the one promised to the two disgruntled boosters.

The regional semifinal against Ignatius would be played at Gund Arena in front of a sold-out crowd of 20,000 fans. It was part of a double header with the Eagles and Wildcats playing in the first game and LeBron James and St. Vincent-St. Mary playing Warrensville in the nightcap in the Division II regional.

They ended up beating Ignatius, 72-58, in the regional. So they had beaten the Cats twice, won the district championship, and eventually ended up going to the final four.

"I never heard from those two guys again," Coach Flannery said. "We were very happy and emotional about the win, and we advanced in the tournament."

So they were to move on to Toledo and play St. John's in the regional championship game. St. John's was 25-0 and ranked No.1 in the state. The Titans had defeated the Eagles by close to 30 earlier in the season.

"I do remember preparing for that game," Coach Flannery said. "We were breaking down film and talking about a lot of things that we had done poorly in that game, missing free throws and missing layups. Sure enough, we were leading St. John's almost the entire game."

The Titans came back and tied it with under a minute to go. With 20 seconds to go, St. Ed's came down the court with the ball, held it, and kicked it out to Neil Frohnapple, who hit a three at the buzzer to enable the Eagles to win by three, 64-61.

Fans were storming the floor. St. John's had 6,000 people there, and St. Ed's had only 1,000 because the game had been played in Toledo.

"A lot of people expected us to lose because they were really good," Coach Flannery said. "To that point that was my biggest accomplishment. As much as the state championship was big, this was the best run I had ever had as a coach."

Donnie O'Toole, a St. Ed's assistant coach, was at the end of the bench. O'Toole is now one of the voices of St. Ed's basketball on internet radio along with Adam Mendoza. O'Toole, whose brother Sean is currently the St. Ignatius head coach, sprinted up the court with both hands up and did a victory lap. He had never experienced this type of run, so he was excited.

At the end of the game, the players and coaches shook hands and the Eagles were handed their trophy.

"We were in the locker room after the game and talking about the post game and what we have to do next and sure enough one of the other assistants comes in and says Coach O'Toole is hooked up to an EKG machine," Flannery explained. "He's in the other room and paramedics are looking at him. We go from this jubilation to everyone bringing it in to say a prayer for Coach O'Toole. I went to the next room and sure enough he was hooked up to an EKG. He had been so excited from running around that he almost passed out. He hyperventilated and was underneath the stands at the end of the game. Someone saw him turning blue because he couldn't catch his breath. In one of the biggest games of our lives, he almost died running around the court."

The story gets better. The good friend and health teacher Flannery is, he was sitting next to Coach O'Toole on the bus on the way back to Cleveland and told him, "Donnie, as a friend, you really have to watch your weight a little bit and get in shape and watch what you are doing. You have a family now and you have to take care of yourself," to which O'Toole replied, "Yes, you are right, you are right." Then Coach Flannery turned to the bus driver and asked him to turn into McDonald's. He then asked Donnie O'Toole what he wanted from McDonald's.

"The last thing you said was that you gave me this true inspirational speech about being in shape, and then two minutes later you offer me something from McDonald's," O'Toole said.

In the state semis, St. Ed's was to play Columbus Brookhaven, which had six Division-I college basketball players on its team. Carney had banked a three-pointer in the last 20 seconds of the game and the Eagles took it to overtime. They lost in overtime, and Brookhaven went on to win the state championship in a blowout.

"It was a team and a run we will never forget," Coach Flannery said. "It wasn't just one game and it wasn't as if we were the No. 1 or 2 team in the state doing it. We beat some teams along the way who were better than us. It goes back to our philosophy. I talked about what it meant to be a great teammate instead of winning with the X's and O's. I mentioned it before, but that was the first team that bought into a philosophy, and the first time that I had sold that philosophy. Did it have something to do with winning and losing? Yes, I would be lying if it didn't. The fact that we made a run verified to me that we could do it again. I had backed up what I had said in the beginning of the season."

He might not have had student-athletes that were as talented as the other teams before that; and yet they still had made it that far. They had Samario Clancy, but they weren't as deep and talented as many of the other teams prior to that. Some of those teams never got out of the districts. Here's a team that had made it to the final four, and had taken the state champ to overtime.

"We were a point away or maybe a basket away from winning the state championship," Coach Flannery said.

Some say Coach Flannery might have been "lucky" when he came in (1996-1997) because of the depth of talent he had had, a base from which he would eventually formulate his philosophy of earning, buying in, and taking ownership regardless of talent level. He'll be the first to admit that might be true.

"There's no question, it was the foundation of where we are today," Coach Flannery said. "That was a great team to have for an extended level.

I was blessed and I know that. I was fortunate to come into a situation in which we had talent, a lot of talent. We were put on the map so to speak, and people were saying, 'Now, St. Ed's is good in basketball.'"

Having talent early had opened up a lot of doors for Flannery in his career. Going to the state championship tournament in 2001-2002 gave him a lot of confidence and might have relieved some pressure because they had already won a state championship.

"To me that adds pressure, because now where do I go?" he conversely said. "I'm measuring myself at such a high standard right from the beginning. Every year I want to win a state championship. I think our program is based on building a culture of success, based on winning and earning a state championship title. It started in '96. Those three ('96-'97-'98) years going back to back really instilled the culture. We had some tough times right after that. In 1999-2000-2001 we struggled. We had to reestablish and redo some things. We had some good players, but we weren't as good as we had been in '96-'97-'98.

"Those years after winning the state built my character as a coach more than the years we won it. I had to learn how to do things differently, how to adapt, how to rebuild our program into a winning program, and build some tradition. I wasn't going to win with talent, and I wasn't going to win just because we are St. Ed's. Part of that early success spoiled me, but the couple years after brought me back to reality. There was a time that I thought that even though I had won a state championship and had had some success, I didn't want to coach any more. I had kids who just thought they were going to be good because they were at St. Ed's due to the success of the kids that had come before them. They never gelled together. I take the blame for it. I wasn't as good a coach as I thought I was. I probably learned a lot more from the years we struggled than I did from the years we were good."

Like the 2013-14 team, that 2001-02 team could be one that was truly worthy of the jersey because it did more than its talent level dictated.

Chapter 20

Getting Worthier During Tournament Clean-up Time

After winning the tough battle against VASJ in 2014, the next three games were fairly easy games for the Eagles, although two of them would be post-season tournament games. In each of the first two playoff games, the Eagles would be without either Nichols or Hamilton. Nichols was banged up in the VASJ game and had also been nursing another injury. As was demonstrated in the pre-season and during the California trip, this team had enough depth to still win without its starters or stars.

First, they had to complete the regular season. They had to make up the Firestone game from earlier in the season that had been postponed because of school closings due to weather conditions.

The Eagles finished the regular season undefeated at home by trouncing Firestone, 83-40. They would enter the playoffs with a 19-2 record, one win shy of the school record for the regular season.

For the second home game in a row, Coach Flannery went with an all-senior starting lineup. All nine seniors on the team scored.

"We were able to get the reserves some minutes and get guys some opportunities to score," Coach Flannery said. "Those guys have been practicing all year and deserved some time. In my brutal honesty in the beginning of the season, I had told the guys that I didn't think we could win 19 or 20 games with our schedule."

Meyer, who hadn't had many starts in his career and had been the sixth and seventh man all year, started on this night and scored a team-high 16 points.

The Eagles would get a bye in the first round of the playoffs as the No. 1 seed and then get a home game for the sectional championship against Valley Forge. The Eagles would capture their 18th sectional championship in the last 19 years with an 81-28 conquest of Forge.

Only 15 of 18 players on the varsity roster could dress because of tournament rules, so the injured Funderburk along with Parente and Nichols were in street clothes. Of the 15 Eagles who did dress, 14 scored at least one point.

Ryan had a game-high 14 points, marking the first time he led the team in scoring.

The next game would be in the district semifinal in Broadview Heights as the tournament moved to neutral courts. In a game in which the Eagles led by as many as 35 points, they routed Nordonia, 69-37. The Eagles once again had more than ten players who scored in double figures.

Team bonding had really shown in this game and again provided more evidence of how strong the St. Ed's bench was and how much of an impact it could have on a game. In the second half when the Eagles were on offense with a rather comfortable lead and Nordonia refused to play defense, the entire St. Ed's bench had become vocal as the five players on the floor decided to hold the ball until the Knights were ready to do something. They were getting into it for their teammates. Finally one of the most unusual things happened: one of the officials stopped the game and walked over to talk to Coach Flannery.

"They were yelling at our bench for talking," Coach Flannery explained. "It is the first time that has ever happened. I couldn't be prouder of my team for getting that warning because I am always telling my team to make noise on the bench. The referee took it the wrong way, thinking that we were yelling at their players. After I told him that was what I want them to do, it was OK. I told him that if they were being disrespectful to let me know. They weren't."

The incident again indicated how much the depth of the team would be their No. 1 asset and that guy No. 18 was as vital to the success of this team as guy No. 1.

Because the Nordonia defense was in a zone, no one came out to take the point guard. As a result, no five-second call could be made. The Eagles refused to penetrate until they could get a defensive effort.

"We were loud and trying to be energized; we weren't yelling at them (Nordonia's players)," Coach Flannery said. "We encourage our guys on the bench to stay in the game."

The Eagles led by as many as 35 points. Twelve players wound up scoring for St. Ed's that night.

Afterward the St. Ed's players and coaches stayed to watch the Westlake-Brunswick semifinal. What they saw in the eventual winner, Brunswick, was a team that preferred to take three-point shots. The Eagles were to face a team contrary to themselves, who like to pound the ball inside. Defensively, St. Ed's was hoping to use its speed and height to its advantage.

It would not be an easy victory for the Eagles, certainly not one of those games that began 10-0 with St. Ed's in the lead. The Blue Devils made the Eagles work.

Now was the time to learn from that playoff loss one year ago. It was time to come together as a team. It was time to put that bonding generated in California into practice. Against the Blue Devils, the Eagles trailed at halftime, 32-29. Brunswick rode that momentum into the second half, going up 42-35 early in the third quarter. Finally, the Eagles went on a 15-0 run to take a 50-42 lead.

Sometimes big runs happen at the start of games and sometimes in the middle of games. Recalling the mind candy, the Eagles were to "find a way" no matter what the circumstances. No excuses would be made on this night. They had overcome too much during this season to allow Brunswick to get away with anything it had not earned.

The 15-0 run showcased at the district level what so many observers had already seen in the Eagles' Nest and on the road this season.

Many of these points were created off the defense as the pesky Eagles in the front court forced the Blue Devils into numerous mistakes, which were then converted into transition baskets.

"I thought I would take it upon myself," said Walters, who had three steals and a game-high eight assists. "I don't like it when teams put a lot of points on us and think of us as easy to get by. I took it upon myself to create havoc. I was getting them to think way too much and pressuring them as much as I could."

In the midst of that 15-0 run, Walters scored a pivotal basket. Hamilton had just scored off an assist from Vuyancih to make it 42-42. On the ensuing inbound pass by the Blue Devils, Walters stole the ball and scored to make it, 44-42, with 3:07 to go in the third quarter.

"It was a really big momentum change," Walters explained. "I saw my teammates getting up and I decided to pick up the defensive pressure. It (Hamilton's basket) had motivated me to play some defense. I saw the ball and I took it and I just had to score."

Nichols scored a game-high 24 points, dished off six assists, and had three steals. Nichols had missed a couple games, nursing a bad hip and an ailing knee, but this night he was effective all over the floor.

"This has seemed to be a trend over the last few games," Nichols said. "We just pick up the defense. We go in at halftime and we make some adjustments. Coach Flan is one of the greatest at doing that in this whole country. We just put the pressure on the other team and made them feel uncomfortable."

Brunswick's bread-and-butter is the three-point shot and on this night the Devils had eight from beyond the arc. Vuyancih was assigned to guard Ryan Badowski, one of the top three-point shooters on the team.

"In the first quarter, we had a lot of high energy on defense, but then it went down," Vuyancih said. "Throughout the second half we had the energy we needed on defense. Transition points off the defense win a lot of games and we scored a lot of them. I am the guy coach wants to guard those kinds of players. I know him (Badowski) personally; he is a great shooter. I had to take away his shooting game."

Also key on defense was Ryan, who had had two booming rejections in the first half and quite an offensive night during which he scored a baker's dozen.

"We had to block shots and stop the scoring of Badowski and a couple other guys," Ryan said. "Sometimes I don't get the ball a lot inside, but I did tonight and I like being both the offensive and defensive threat."

After cutting down the nets following the game, the Eagles immediately focused on the regional and a third date with arch-rival St. Ignatius.

Now 22-2, the Eagles were to play Ignatius in the first round of the regional in the James A. Rhodes Arena (JAR) at the University of Akron. An adage has it that beating a team three times in one season is one of the toughest things to accomplish in sports, but it is still a myth. Three times in the previous 20 years St. Ed's has defeated St. Ignatius thrice in one season. Still fresh in their minds was the overtime game in Ohio City and what had happened in the next game.

The Eagles received the surprise news that Funderburk would return sooner than expected. The No. 2 center returned to the lineup for the St. Ignatius game. Funderburk had missed a couple games early in the season and had returned for that first game in California against SunnySlope. Then, his return was uneventful as he had four fouls and zero points in that game. Now the question was what impact would his return have in the playoffs.

"His coming back absolutely played a big part in our run," Coach Flannery said. "We had started playing well without him. We were adding depth, and a 6-foot-9 guy, whom other people could not readily counter. The team was uplifted. If Kipper or Mike Ryan were not playing well or in foul trouble, we had Derek.

"Any time we get a player back, it makes everyone feel more confident. Whether he sees it or not, it helped everyone else to play well when he played and he played a lot. It's another element of why we were good. On the other side, a guy like Mike Ryan could have done the same thing. Mike was playing really well in the playoffs."

While Funderburk was to play a big factor eventually in the championship game, he was also huge in the regional tournament. He split time at center with Ryan, who was still the starter. Since the coaching staff wanted to take it slow with Funderburk, he played only five minutes against Ignatius, but he made his presence known with a blocked shot. Ryan, on the other hand, had two blocked shots, playing remarkably on defense.

"Ignatius is standing between us and a state championship; they just happen to be the team standing there right now," Coach Flannery had said a couple days before the game. "We try not to make it bigger than it is. It is always going to be tougher to beat teams the more times we play them because of familiarity. They have a sense of what we do."

The Eagles had to guard against what St. Ignatius had done in the first two games, pushing them to the outside and forcing long outside shots.

"We are a much more effective team when we are able to take the ball to the basket, but they have the size (to defend it and coax the Eagles to go outside their game), with the Black brothers (Eric and David)," Coach Flannery said. "They have athleticism and depth. We can't naturally wear them down."

Regardless of what the Wildcats had done the first two times, St. Ed's worked on playing smart during practice that week.

"I don't know if they were taking it (the drive to the hoop) away from us as much as they were just clogging the lanes on us," Coach Flannery said in a pre-game interview. "We get a 10-0 lead, we start taking some jump shots and then we start missing them. We became comfortable not attacking the basket and not doing what we do well. We became a different team through our own stupidity in a sense. We are going to have to knock down some threes and perimeter shots because of their size and athleticism."

The crowd came out in full force. A total of 2,830 flew through the turnstiles for the game. Most notable was the St. Ed's student section. There were two such sections for this game. One section was underneath the basket and another behind the St. Ed's bench. By now, many were wearing their "Bench Mob" T-shirts in full appreciation of the important role depth had had in this season's success.

Hamilton emerged as a statistical leader, nearly attaining a triple double by scoring nine points, grabbing ten rebounds, and dishing off seven assists. Walters scored a career-high and game-high 16 points, as the Eagles downed the Cats, 70-59. By halftime, the Eagles had been in command, leading 37-19. It was another one of those games in which the Eagles had started with a big burst, opening up a 13-1 lead at the game's onset.

"Most of the games we have won this year have started with the D in the first quarter," Hamilton later said in the press conference. "We figured that if we played with a lot of intensity, we could force them to make bad decisions."

Remaining level headed, the players kept in mind that it could only happen by being mindful that one part of the team is as important as any other part.

"I got those points because guys like him were passing the ball well," Walters said as he pointed to Hamilton.

Coach Flannery agreed. "Putting Marsalis in the middle of the floor against a team that starts to trap makes it easy as a coach," Coach Flannery said. "He makes great decisions. He's underrated as a passer. He has great knowledge of the game. Kids who play for me at St. Ed's are overlooked because they are unselfish."

Nichols added 13 points and Meyer came off the bench to add 14.

"They have a lot of guys who get easy buckets, but if we get them in foul trouble, they don't have as many guys who can get those easy buckets," said St. Ignatius Head Coach Sean O'Toole. "St. Ed's is extremely well coached and talented. We were just trying to play a game within a game, trying to set and attain manageable goals. There's a reason that team has only one loss in Ohio. They are deep, share the ball well, and attack well. The key is to get the Nicholses and Hamiltons off the floor. I am happy there are no more Hamiltons at St. Ed's. Between him and his brother (Myles), they were something. The kid really carries this team. Also, Vuyancih and Walters are no slouches with the way they hit their threes. They have a good bench."

Half of the regional was played in Lima, Ohio, where Mansfield had emerged as the next opponent for St. Ed's in a game to be played in the JAR.

"As hard as it was facing that team for a third time, this was going to make it that much more special. We could say we not only won the state championship, but we beat our arch rival three times," Coach Flannery later said.

While Funderburk's return had been a big spark for the playoffs, the No. 1 center, Ryan, had also shone in the tournament run.

Ryan had improved throughout the season as much as anybody. He could score; he could rebound. He could do a lot of things that a lot of people cannot do.

"Because of Kipper and Marsalis, he did not have to do all those things," Coach Flannery said. "He was one of those unsung heroes. He's a solid, fundamental basketball player. It's great to have that kind of kid on our team, one who doesn't get much exposure but could still potentially be a D-I basketball player. If he's playing at any other school, he could be scoring 20 or 25 points a game and be a high-profile player."

The junior started the 2012-13 season as a sophomore spending half time on the varsity and half time on the JV team. That did not last very long as he was promoted to full-time varsity within the first months of the season. He had become worthy of the jersey rather quickly by earning it.

"Mike is my favorite story," JV Coach Josh Nugent said. "Mike played as a freshman for me on the freshman team. He made the jump very few people make; he jumped right from freshman to varsity. He skipped the JV step. He started the sophomore year and played one or two games with us (the JV team) for a few quarters, but by the fourth or fifth game of the year he was already full-time varsity. Mike is a testament to a player needing to earn his spot. He really made a leap. His leap from his sophomore year to junior year has been great as well. We expect a similar leap for him from junior to senior year."

While the defense had been ever present from the onset against Ignatius, it would need to be intact against Mansfield, which also came into the game with a reputation for stellar defense. In the Tygers' regional semifinal win, they had held Bowsher to 50 points. Bowsher had reached 100 points eight times during the season.

Mansfield had advanced to the Elite Eight for the first time since 2004-2005. The last time the Tygers had done so they beat a St. Ed's team in the regional semi, 76-55, at the University of Toledo in 2005.

If the Tygers were to do what they did against Bowsher, they had to limit St. Ed's to only one shot or get a defensive stop each time they went on defense. The Eagles would have to make the most of each offensive possession, get offensive rebounds and score their put-backs. Both Ryan and Meyer had been strong on the put-backs this season.

Led by Ryan, St. Edward received the defensive effort it needed while at the same time denying the Tygers the defensive game they desired, while pounding out a 74-57 win.

Ryan had a game-high four blocked shots. He added 12 points and seven rebounds. He shared game-high honors in rebounds with Nichols and Hamilton. The win put the Eagles at 24-2, two games away from not only winning the state championship but tying the school record for most wins in a season.

"This is a great St. Ed's program and this was well deserved," Mansfield Head Coach J.T. Reese said. "We were expecting to guard them better, and we didn't do that."

St. Ed's outrebounded the Tygers, 38-26, including 28-15 on offense. The Eagles were getting more efficient, as they shot well 67 percent from the field in the first half and 58.7 percent for the game. For the game, the Eagles shot 70 percent from the foul line and 60 percent from behind the arc.

"It felt good to have a good game before we go down to the final four in Columbus," Vuyancih said. "Going down to Columbus is an amazing thing to start off, but one thing to keep in mind is the moment we lost (62-51 to Whitmer in the final four in 2012), I looked at my hand and thought I was very close to getting a ring and winning a state championship for our school. That was one of the worst feelings I ever had. We don't want to feel like that again."

While building that big first-half lead, the Eagles were perfect from three-point territory, on 4-of-4, including two by Vuyancih, who scored a game-high 19 points.

Vuyancih's fellow senior, Hamilton, was one of three to reach double figures in scoring with 10. For the second time in three nights, he flirted with a triple double, grabbing seven rebounds and passing off six assists. It all had come down to putting the team first and making the sacrifices necessary to be a state championship team.

"The last couple weeks Marsalis has been more unselfish and more of the senior leader we always thought he could be," Coach Flannery said in the press conference after the game. "It's not that he hasn't been all year; it's just that lately there has been more of a sense of urgency for him. He's showing that on the floor by scoring when he has to but also by being a leader in distributing the ball when he has to."

Nineteen of St. Edward's 27 field goals had been assisted.

A rematch between St. Ed's and Shaker Heights was not to be as the Red Raiders were eliminated from the playoffs in the regional. Instead, the Eagles would oppose another Cleveland area team in East Tech. Thus, the Eagles, who had started the regular season with a team from the Senate Athletic Conference, would start the final four with another team from the Senate.

All the rage around the Cleveland area was about East Tech. The Scarabs had a storied history in track and basketball in Cleveland, dating back to the 1930s. It is the alma mater of Olympic gold medalists Harrison Dillard and Jesse Owens.

"We had played a similar team to East Tech in the final four in '98 when we played Withrow in the semis," Coach Flannery said in a teleconference the week of the game. "They were a city team from Cincinnati that hadn't been there (to the final four) for forever and they were trying to build a new gym. They had their whole community behind them – almost an identical story to East Tech."

Led by Lawrence Bolden, his nephew Antonio Bolden, and Jim Abrams, East Tech had won the state championship in 1972 and hadn't been back to the final four since then. During that time East Tech had been the most dominant program around the Cleveland area in the early '70s. St. Ed's also had a decent program led by the high-scoring Rod Dieringer.

Even though this was 2014, the buzz around Cleveland was that this East Tech team was trying to live off that legacy. In fact, some of the players on the 2014 team were related to some of those on the 1972 team.

Much like Mansfield, East Tech would play a game with more than two guards on the floor, including five at times. This game would pit speed versus size.

"A lot of the games in our league are like a track meet so this (playing against a team that pounds the ball inside) will be different for us," East Tech Coach Brett Moore said the week of the game in a press teleconference.

The Eagles used their size to their advantage. Ryan had had a superb game on both ends of the floor against Mansfield in the regional final, and the 6-9 Funderburk had been a strong presence in the middle in the 18 minutes he was able to play against the Tygers. The increased minutes from the Ignatius game for Funderburk had prepared him for the final four in which he would play a key factor.

"D.J. is a high major player who was getting into his stride midway through the season until he broke his foot," Coach Flannery said in the teleconference. "We thought he was through for the season, but there was a slight chance he could come back. The doctor did some things to help his recovery so that when they took his cast off two weeks ago, he was healed."

The Eagles would be at an advantage since they had seen a similar team less than one week earlier.

"They are very similar to Mansfield although they are a little more talented than Mansfield," Coach Flannery said. "We played a couple teams in California with three or four guards. We have had experience in playing those kinds of teams, but they are scary."

Realizing how hard it is to get a team to the final four and subsequently win a state championship, Coach Flannery was beginning to recollect the first state championship and that it had been 16 years since that time. He realized what a gift he had now.

"Back then I thought it was easy," Coach Flannery said. "Over the years I have learned how hard it is to get there and win. I now appreciate that. It is true that nothing could be taken away from experience. This team's talent is more than I anticipated. We have been getting the most of their talent. We don't lose a beat in terms of talent when we go to our bench. Tony and Marsalis have taken this team, grabbed them, and said, 'We want to win the state championship.'"

Both Hamilton (four-year varsity student-athlete) and Vuyancih came off the bench for the last St. Ed's team to make it to the final four (2011-2012). Myles Hamilton, his older brother who plays for Kennesaw State, had been one of the primary components of that team.

While Marsalis Hamilton had two excellent games statistically in the regional tournament with 19 points, 17 rebounds and 13 assists, he struggled at the start of the state semifinal game against East Tech. He played only three minutes of the first half against Tech, committing three fouls and four turnovers and scoring no points. He sat out the rest of the first half after garnering his third foul.

"We could see it in Marsalis," Coach Flannery would explain later. "His brother had most of the success back in 2012. Marsalis felt like he was the guy who was going to win the state championship for St. Ed's. He was just trying to do too much. He was trying to score; he was trying to create. Other teams knew he would do that. He ended up turning over the ball early on and getting into foul trouble. He took a couple bad shots. He needs to know he is a great player and great passer, and he can do so many things. He is not going to determine the final outcome of the game in the first minute by scoring a basket."

As a team captain and leader, he needed to get everyone involved and let the game come to him and see how it was to develop, Hamilton would later admit.

"Once he saw that, he calmed down, started making some passes, and started playing better defense," Coach Flannery said. "He had a couple rebounds and got into to the flow of the game. He had an incredible run early in the second half. He let the game come to him. He wasn't forcing shots. The regional games were indicators of what Marsalis could do. He was rebounding, scoring and passing. He understands the game, but there's also his passing ability. He's able to find that guy in some of the most unique situations."

At that early point of the game, Tech had the momentum. "We felt very good about our chances once we got to that point (of Hamilton allowing the game to come to him)," Coach Flannery said.

Without Hamilton, the Bench Mob had its say, as the Eagles had built a 20-point lead by halftime, 43-23. Hamilton came out in the second half a much different person. In 11 minutes in the second half, he scored seven points with four assists and five rebounds.

"After the East Tech game, coach talked to me and I agreed with him," Hamilton would later say. "I didn't let the game come to me. I was trying to take it, rushing into things."

In a rout, the Eagles disposed of the Scarabs, 89-64, led by Nichols' game-high 25 points. As far as the Bench Mob went, even with Hamilton having a cool night, the Eagles still had five double-figure scorers. Vuyancih had 10, while Meyer came off the bench to score 14, and Funderburk came off the pines to score 12.

Thanks to fast healing, Funderburk was able to have an impact on this final four. In 14 minutes, he also had four rebounds and a steal. As for the point-guard situation that had been a concern at the start of the season, Walters directed the offense well with a game-high seven assists.

The efficiency of the team continued to improve with this game. The Eagles outrebounded the Scarabs, 37-20, including a 28-5 advantage on the defensive boards. For the game, the Eagles shot 71 percent from the field while Tech shot only 39 percent. From three-point territory, St. Ed's shot 66 percent and Tech 30 percent. From the line, the Eagles shot 90 percent and the Scarabs 48 percent.

Thirty-three of the 89 points had come from the bench.

"The bench has been really important, which is why we are one of the best teams in the state if not the best," Nichols said in the press conference after the game. "Consistently, Will has been bringing a spark off the bench every night. When one man struggles, the bench is there to pick him up. We pride ourselves on defense, getting stops and getting the other team uncomfortable. We've been smart in the half court and playing our game."

The Bench Mob by now was earning recognition around the state.

"I am sure some of the guys this year heard this: 'You guys are just on the team. You don't really play a lot. Are you going to get in?'" said Brian Ansberry, the former St. Ed's assistant coach. "They're just busting their chops. They might see some friends from their own neighborhood that they might be better than. Pisco, an Avon Lake kid, might have been a starter if he would have gone to Avon Lake High School.

"I tell players that I am coaching now. I say, 'Listen do you want to be part of something bigger than yourself?' I see it all the time in the paper, kids scoring 28 points for a team that is not that good. I always point that out. I do stat research and in Flannery's era there have been only a couple guys who have averaged over 20 a game (at St. Ed's). It's because the teams are so good. At some of these schools, a guy is averaging 30 points a game because he is the only guy on the team. I would say without a doubt, I wouldn't trade it. I would rather be a bench guy who doesn't play a whole lot that might not get the headlines but say that I was on a state title team. I was on that team, played with those guys, practiced against them. Just as Connor echoed."

The Eagles had 22 turnovers while the Scarabs had only 17.

"We did a decent job of taking care of the ball tonight, but not quite as well as I would have liked," Coach Flannery said after the game.

Also pivotal off the bench was Riley, who had given the Eagles their first double-digit lead, and the double-digit lead for good by hitting a three from the corner with 3:26 to go in the first quarter with an assist from Nichols to make it 17-6.

"We were knocking down shots and it says a lot for the focus of this team in wanting to get things done," Coach Flannery said in the press conference. "My guys are so obnoxious and cocky in wanting to do it for me. We were up 30, and I was yelling at the assistant coaches, asking them if we were still ahead. I'm on pins and needles and these guys are telling me to be relaxed. That's just the makeup of this team this year. They are backing up what their talk has been."

The Bench Mob on the bench for the team received support from the Bench Mob in the stands as two buses of students made it to the game.

"Since he hasn't won a state title in 16 years, we want to do this for Coach Flan," Meyer, one of the Bench-Mob leaders, said moments after the win. "We want to get it done tomorrow. It's great that they have been out to support us. They (the student section) are a big help. They have been there for us all year at our home games, and now they are here."

Now there was one game left to prove that they were truly worthy of the jersey.

Chapter 21

The Final Goal Accomplished, Truly Worthy of the Jersey

Having eliminated East Tech, the Eagles faced Upper Arlington in the state championship game. Arlington had eliminated Trotwood Madison, 74-49, to get to the final game. In his seventh final-four appearance, this would be Coach Flannery's third state championship game. The leaders would take ownership and play a big role.

Vuyancih had been a vocal leader in both his junior and senior years as a captain. Now he took ownership of that leadership role. On the night before the Upper Arlington game, Vuyancih summoned the rest of the team to his hotel room for a players' only meeting. Coach Flannery had not known what was said in that meeting but at the time was confident that it was productive.

"My dad (Pat Vuyancih) would always talk to me about leadership, giving me tips here and there," Vuyancih said. "He told me that his team at Cleveland State had a meeting before the Sweet 16 game (against David Robinson's Navy after having upset Bobby Knight's Indiana) about what was going on that night and what they could and could not do among themselves as players. Whenever we had meetings with Coach Flan, and they all loved Coach Flan, but we would hear the same voice over and over again. It doesn't sink in as much any more, so I thought that bringing the guys together and restating it coming from us would be helpful. That's something that Coach Flan always told us. 'It's not going to come from the coaches; it's going to come from you guys.' We sat down and it really came from us. We talked about how we are doing it for one another, but the No. 1 thing was to make this memory. We are doing it for the entire community, and we're doing it for Coach Flan and our families too.

"It was basically reminding one another. None of us got into one another's faces. It wasn't too relaxed, but it was relaxed. We just had a conversation among ourselves, basically telling one another to get focused, do whatever they needed to do to get focused -- superstitions before the game, get to bed on time, etc. Do everything the normal way and be comfortable and ready to go."

While doing it for their coach, they knew it came from the top. They had bought into the concept of earning their roles, sharing/bonding with one another, sacrificing for the team, and having collective responsibility. It had started even before the Vuyancih players' only meeting.

"On the whole way down on the bus, we talked about winning the championship," Walters said. "We talked about having the meeting while on the bus. We first came in and were joking around and then it became really serious. Tony told me and everyone else how serious this was. We all came in there and said our peace and said that this was going to be a team win. We can't do this individually. We had to come together strong as a team instead of doing our own thing. Everybody was on the same page. The people who didn't play that much had our backs, and that showed how much on the same level we were. That was the final piece that we needed."

Player No. 18's importance would shine just as much as player No. 1's.

"We knew we could get it done," Pisco said. "Even the night before, Tony called a meeting before the semifinal game. The next night we got together again, so we had two meetings back-to-back. We all just talked about what we needed to do. In the end, it came down to just playing hard and doing what St. Ed's basketball is. I feel like that's what we accomplished in those games." Added Parente, "Even at the beginning of the meeting we were goofing around. Someone said something about how we owe it to Coach Flan. He's given us everything that we need to win."

Captain Riley, the head of the Bench Mob, said, "Going into the season and throughout the mind candy and the meetings, it was everyone's ultimate goal to win the state championship. We didn't hear anyone say that my goal is to score 20 points in a game. Everyone wanted to collectively win a state championship. Looking back 10 years from now, we are not going to say I remember when I had 25 points against Ignatius. We are going to remember that we won the state championship our senior year of high school. We'll never play for St. Ed's again, and we'll want to go out with having done something worthy."

Nichols became inspired by the meeting and would follow with a career night the next day.

"The meeting was serious and goofy at the same time," Nichols said. "We're so close that it didn't even matter. In the grand scheme of things, the meeting helped big time. It was about us getting our focus before the big game. We knew what we came down there for; and some people's minds might have been somewhere else but Tony, being the leader, called us all and we rallied together."

The mind candy the next night excerpted from Deuteronomy (see Chapter Four on mind candy and Chapter Five for the Bible passage) had inspired the players to know that they had a higher purpose.

"I remember seeing that one, and I was kind of surprised that it was brought up," Vuyancih said. "I don't think I was really ready for it. I was happy seeing it. We're a Catholic school, and we have to end this on a Catholic-type note. That's what we are here for; it is a reminder that we are doing it for God. We are using our talents for Him. We are so blessed to be here."

Prior to the East Tech game and prior to the Upper Arlington game, the players wore T-shirts that said, "Soaring for Big Mike" and NEGU (Never Ever Give Up). It was in honor of Mike Orbany, and it inspired the players.

"I was able to have a good game by staying humble and staying in God, because there are a lot of people (such as Orbany) that would kill to be in my position," Nichols said. "Don't waste it. Don't waste the blessing that God gave.

"It's a great group of guys and a great coaching staff and I love them to death. If I had to do it all over again, I would have done the same thing.

Last year it was kind of what is going on? It was rough. That's why I thank God. God is so good. I could have been somewhere else, where the outcome wouldn't have been as great. God is just good. His plan is better than ours. Everything worked out for the best."

Upper Arlington was a team much like St. Ed's – playing unselfish ball, taking good care of the ball, playing good defense, and taking smart shots.

"Playing a team like ours that plays good defense and takes care of the ball was different because we hadn't played too many teams like that," Walters said.

Arlington moved the ball around well and used a lot of back cuts to get inside, easy baskets.

"There are several concerns but the biggest thing is that they are a hard team to prepare for in the little time that we have in terms of X's and O's," Coach Flannery said during that Saturday afternoon's (just a few hours prior to the start of the game) practice at Bishop Hartley High School. "We have to rely on mostly what we have been taught all year about how to defend certain screens and the back cuts. They are a patient basketball team."

Had the Eagles drawn Trotwood Madison instead of Arlington, it would have been easier for them to prepare since Madison ran offenses and defenses similar to both East Tech and Mansfield. That would have made it a natural transition, but instead it became problematic to prepare for in such a short time for both the players and coaches.

Nugent produced the scouting report and began the discussion at practice that afternoon.

"He (Coach Flannery) confidently said when we win Friday have something ready for me Saturday," Coach Nugent said. "Coaches (Jason) Bratten, (Tim) Smith and I got together as much information as we could on Upper Arlington and Trotwood Madison coming in to the tournament. We were hoping for Trotwood Madison on one end because they were very similar to Mansfield Senior and East Tech. We could have applied the principles we used for those two teams. Upper Arlington one could imagine was a nightmare to prepare for; they (the Golden Bears) were so good at what they did.

"At the same time, we remembered being down there in 2008, and we probably had gone a little overboard trying to prepare for the state championship game against Newark. The kids just need to know what is needed of them to make it work. If all of a sudden we are changing who we are or changing how we prepare, it starts to fall. Even the kids can sense it. They'll say, 'We've never prepared like this before.' We were very deliberate in getting the keys to what we wanted. We stayed up that night and figured the things the kids needed to know. We probably needed three days to get ready for Upper Arlington, but the kids just needed those 10 minutes to understand what they were about, who their key players were, how they were going to try to score, and what they might do to us defensively. Then we had to go out and execute."

While the one-to-18 concept had worked so well for the Eagles thus far, it didn't mean that other teams couldn't have the same mindset, with players who had earned their roles and bought into the basics, etc. Certainly St. Ed's was not that unique that it wouldn't also meet someone along the way that had also done all the right things. With only two left standing, it came down to who wanted it the most and which team would have its best game. Still there was that one trait of Upper Arlington that no other St. Ed's opponents had had this season. This made it more difficult for scouts like Coach Nugent to come back with the right formula.

"They are different from most things we have seen all year," Coach Flannery said. "Some teams try to play some one-on-one and isolate us and use their athleticism and talent. Upper Arlington plays literally like a team."

What everyone would learn by the end of the game and during the following week was how efficient both teams would be in this manner. It would not be a matter of merely taking advantage of the others' mistakes. Teams this good just don't make too many mistakes.

"In the back of our minds, we understood what Upper Arlington was going to do," said Tom Bodle, the assistant coach. "We had played a team in California that was a lot like Upper Arlington. They used the shot clock (which is used in high school ball in the Golden State). There were a couple times they put the limit on it. We had to get used to playing hard defense for 30 or 40 seconds. A lot of teams will play defense for 10 seconds and then they go to the back door to get the easy layup. That was Upper Arlington's strength. They were patient enough that teams would collapse their defense, but we didn't. We had been working on that in practices all year just in case we would see that."

A low-scoring affair certainly was not out of the question. The Eagles had had a game in California in which the combined score of the two teams did not reach 100.

"The good thing about our team is that we have played different styles," Coach Flannery explained the day of the game. "We have played in low-scoring games. We have done well against teams that play that way. That's a possibility. If we can play up tempo, we'll have a better chance of winning. However, we don't want to give up easy baskets just to control the pace. We just have to concentrate on getting good stops on defense."

In the semifinal victory against East Tech, the Eagles made 33 of the 46 shots for a 71.7 field goal shooting percentage.

"If we shoot that well, we will win, but that is hard to do," Coach Flannery said. "I want us to continue to shoot well from the free-throw line. We can't rely on being a 70-percent shooting team; we have to play good defense and rebound well while we are doing it. We have to realize that today is a different day."

The shooting was even better against East Tech at the free-throw line, where the Eagles made 19-of-21 for better than 90 percent.

Coach Delvon Blanton has been coaching the big guys for four years. During that time, they had some good teams. However, this team was special and had the bonding like few others at the school that translated into the confidence to go all the way.

"Of all the years I have been there, this team here I could see it from day one," Coach Blanton said. "The love, the like, the care and respect for one another. You could see we had something special because each of those 18 kids would die for one another. The last couple years, the last couple teams did not have that same feel. They didn't love and care for one another like this team did. I used to like to tell them in the circle every game, 'You guys are special.' I could see it. I could feel it. 'You guys could really make something special out of this year.' This wasn't the most talented team at St. Ed's, but it was the most joyous to coach. They listened, and they worked hard for one another. There was never any bickering or complaining about not playing much. They all showed up and worked hard every day in practice. This is what they got. Flan is a heck of a coach because he touches them and he reaches them. They can call on him at any time. Other coaches might care about the basketball part, but after basketball they won't hear from them any more. Flan is different. That's what brought me to him."

The student body's support would play a critical role in this one since by now they had picked up on the idea that the depth of the team would make the biggest difference.

"The students embracing the whole Bench Mob thing and everyone on the bench being in the game the whole time really showed it wasn't just the first five starters who played or the first eight who played; it was the whole team, the whole players, the whole coaching staff. Everyone played his part," Riley said.

After Saturday's practice at Bishop Hartley, the Eagles returned to the Jerome Schottenstein Center's Value City Arena for everything they had been building toward all year – the state championship game.

Upper Arlington was only a few miles from Value City Arena so it was easy for the Golden Bears to attract a lot of fans to the game for support. The Golden Bears drew 14,322 fans in the semifinal against Trotwood Madison while the St. Ed's-East Tech game had only 9,890. The word buzzing around town the afternoon of the championship game was that it would again be a crowd of more than 14,000 and might be the largest ever for a state championship game and might even sell out.

"Everything we went through throughout the season was needed in the state championship," Coach Flannery was later to say. "The travel, the camaraderie, the toughness, and the high-efficient offense all were needed; we had to play great defensively and we had to be patient. We had to have composure, great leadership, confidence, and get everyone involved – not just the guys on the floor but the guys on the bench. This was to make it a true team effort."

As it turned out, 14,234 fans packed in Value City Arena for the game. Most of them were cheering for Upper Arlington

"I don't think it (the crowd) shook any of us at all," Vuyancih said. "None of us got nervous. We saw all those guys up there, but I think it inspired us a lot more. When we were doing the national anthem, I was looking up and I think it was Malcolm and I and we were just laughing at all these people and I said, 'These are a lot of hearts to break. Let's go out there and do this.'"

Walters took the cue from his teammate and fellow senior captain.

"We heard at the hotel that there were going to be a lot of people, but not that many people," Walters said. "We were used to playing in front of big crowds all year – the California games, the Ignatius games. We were used to the loud atmosphere. The crowd did not affect us."

This was much more than even the biggest crowds the Eagles had played in front of over the past couple years.

"We played games with big crowds like Ignatius and Mater Dei, but there has never been a crowd like that. Before the game they were telling us it was almost sold out," Parente said. "We all got pumped up for that. It was pretty exciting. The whole game it was so loud."

The point guards would have to hold on to the ball and make sure the large crowd would not trigger bad passes or dribbles.

"Throughout our four years at St. Ed's, we have played in front of big crowds, especially with the Silent Night games and the Ignatius games," Riley, the other point guard, said. "During the game we really don't pay attention to them. When we walked into Value City Arena, we looked around and saw almost a packed house. Everyone knew there was going to be a ton of Upper Arlington fans there. Anyone who looked behind our bench could see all the St. Ed's fans and everyone who has been there right from the start. Hearing them throughout the game and hearing them cheer for us picked us up when things were not going well."

Crowd or no crowd, it would not be a pleasant experience for the Eagles in the early going. Contrary to the many games in which the Eagles had jumped out to a quick lead during the season, in this game they would find it done to them. They were down 9-0 before the first quarter was half over. If this were going to happen, it would take one of the best comeback efforts they had to do it.

The Eagles would not score their first points until Hamilton made a layup with 3:36 to go in the first quarter. He was fouled, but missed the shot in attempting to convert on the old-fashioned three-point play. Little by little, the Eagles would convince the Golden Bears that they would not run away with it and would be in for their toughest game of the season. Arlington had lost only one game during the regular season.

"We needed some luck, some big shots and big plays," Coach Flannery said. "I was scared to death because Upper Arlington does so many good things. I felt good about the way my kids played and defended. I didn't keep their composure; they did it themselves. I just told them to do it one possession at a time."

Hamilton's basket would initiate a 10-2 run as the Eagles would pull to within one point, 11-10, by the end of the first quarter, capped by a Nichols layup just before the buzzer sounded. The defense played a big part in this mini comeback with Funderburk and Darien Knowles blocking shots and Nichols turning in a steal.

Still the Eagles could not gain the lead as Arlington remained in control, doing what was expected by the coaching staff, taking their time with the ball, not forcing the shot, and eating time off the clock while keeping the ball out of the hands of the Eagles. It wasn't until 4:49 remained in the half that the Eagles would tie it for the first time, 14-14, on a jump shot by Nichols off the fast break.

While trying to hit the man down low for the layup, the Golden Bears then missed with a layup and the Eagles came down the floor with a chance to take the lead. After a missed shot, Nichols tipped it in and the Eagles had a 16-14 lead with 4:16 to play in the half. While it shifted the momentum, it by no stretch of the imagination meant the Eagles would be able to take command. For the rest of the night, their biggest lead in regulation was two points in a game that saw seven lead changes and eight ties.

On his way to a career night, Nichols tied it at 18 with a layup and then made it a two-point game with a dunk with a half minute to go in the first half. Arlington led, 22-20, at the half.

Things were not comfortable for the Eagles, but it did look a lot better than it had the first four minutes of the game.

Upper Arlington had the lead most of the third quarter but never led by more than five so the Eagles appeared to stay in this one no matter what. After being down 31-26, Ryan's layup pulled the Eagles back to within three. The Eagles tied it twice in the third quarter, making it 26-26 on a three pointer by Nichols and 37-37 on a Funderburk layup. The Eagles had one short lead in the third, 35-34, on another triple by Nichols. Upper Arlington led after three quarters, 40-37, taking the honor of leading at the end of each of the first three quarters.

In the fourth quarter, the lead would go back and forth in the early part of the period, Hamilton had given the Eagles a 41-40 lead with 6:18 to go, but the Golden Bears went on an 8-0 run to take a 48-42 lead with 3:22 to go. At this point, some people might have had doubt, but not the Eagles themselves.

"It is an experience thing," Vuyancih was to say. "When we listen to Coach Flan, he tells us things like, '30 seconds is still a lot of time, guys.' We bought into these things and we believed it. For me, Mike Newton (former St. Ed's point guard) once told me that the second you think you've lost, you've lost. Whether there is five minutes or 30 seconds left in the game; if you do it all the way down to the last second and you believe that you are going to win, there's always that chance that you are going to win. For me, personally, it was always being around these guys. I was always a nervous kind of guy. Kipper, Malcolm and Marsalis were some of the loosest guys I have been around going into a game. They had no worries. They knew they could get it done. Their confidence rubbed off on us, the rest of the team."

So now it was time to dig down deep and draw on all that bonding and recall the one person is as important as the other 17 concept. It was time to buy into unselfish play and earn what one gets.

The Eagles were still down by six points with fewer than two minutes to play. Then the comeback began. A Funderburk layup with 1:54 to go made it 48-44. Funderburk then made three free throws in the next minute to make it 48-47 with 53 seconds left to play. Now was the time to do what the Eagles had done against Ignatius in Sullivan Gymnasium and almost had done on the road at Shaker.

"They found a sense of urgency in the (second) Ignatius game and realized that everything was on the line for the whole year and they didn't want to lose all that in that one night," said Danny Gallagher, who has been an assistant coach with Flannery for eight years. "They found a sense of urgency and found a way to execute offensively and defensively down the stretch against Upper Arlington."

Arlington went back up by three, 50-47, with only 30 seconds left to play. It was time to go to the senior leaders. Vuyancih made a layup with 15 seconds to go to make it 50-49.

Still, it looked bleak when Arlington took a 52-49 lead with 10 seconds to play. It was time for Coach Gallagher, the inbound and special-teams coach, to do his part. St. Ed's called a timeout with four seconds to play and was to inbound from underneath its own basket.

"Danny Gallagher is one of my top guys; he was with me back in high school," Coach Flannery said. "Danny is my blob and slob guy, which is the baseline-out-of-bounds and sideline-out-of-bounds guy. Danny just turned to me with a minute to go and said, 'I have a play for you if you need it.' And I said OK. We'll get to that if we need it. I asked him if it was for a two or three and he said 'a three.' I said OK. With four seconds left we had the ball out of bounds and Danny had the white board with him. He handed the white board to me. I erased it and said, 'Do you have that play?' He said, 'Yeah, but you just erased it.' I took the board and said sorry and here you go. I give him all the credit – even though it was the sixth option on the play – it worked."

Hamilton inbounded the ball to Funderburk, who threw the ball from underneath the basket back on the right wing to Hamilton, who took the shot and made a three as the buzzer sounded, making it 52-52 and sending the game into overtime. Some thought Walters, Nichols, or Vuyancih would take the shot. Coming into the game, Hamilton was only 2-of-9 from behind the arc. He was an unlikely hero on this play. Yet, all the things Hamilton had learned along the way about being an unselfish player and a good leader, finally paid off as he got his chance to shine when it counted the most.

"I was the third option," Hamilton said. "I'll start from the huddle. Coach (Gallagher) was drawing up the play and shaking. He kept drawing and shaking and he looked up to me. I am looking at everyone. We broke the huddle and after we were walking out of the huddle, I said to Derek that 'if nothing works, I am giving it to you.' He already knew to pass it back. Tony came up and wasn't open. Malcolm came off and Kip came off. All of them were crowded. I couldn't turn the ball over. We had to get a shot. I countered and handed off to Derek. The guy gave me an advantage because he jumped to the ball with me.

"The play was designed for Tony and Kipper to get the first two looks. When Tony and Kipper weren't open, Derek looked up at me and just gave it to me. I appreciated that. I took a little dribble and Derek gave the guy a little bump to clear it for me to take the shot. So I took the shot. I let it go and prayed to God that it would go in."

There was still overtime to play, but with the kind of momentum Hamilton's shot had brought the Eagles, there just was no way the Eagles were going to let this one get away from them.

"Finally, Marsalis hits that shot; I don't think anybody thought we were going to lose after that shot," Coach Flannery said. "When that shot went down, coaches, players and everybody believed and knew we were going to win. It was a great journey. A special mention should go to the Bench Mob. I cannot force 18 guys or anybody to buy into liking one another. I can't force people and say, 'Hey guys, be OK with not playing. Be OK with just supporting your teammates.' It doesn't work that way. The kids themselves had to buy into that. These guys bought into that – whether it was early in the season, middle of the season, or late in the season. We don't win it with just Marsalis hitting the shot. It was the support that these guys gave one another. The 18th guy is as important as the first guy. They will never forget this journey – never."

Added Coach Blanton, "In the end, it looked like we were going to lose. When Sal made that shot, I knew we were going to win. Flan kept telling them in the huddle, 'We are going to win.' I could look at every kid in that huddle, and I could see that they believed it."

In overtime, the Eagles gave Arlington a dose of its own medicine. Funderburk won the tip and the Eagles had the ball to start the overtime. Now it was time for Walters to show what a great point guard he had become as the Eagles held the ball.

"We had to take a couple breaths; we started playing the game we know how especially in overtime," Walters said. "In overtime we started really holding the ball. We passed the ball around I don't know how many times until we got a decent shot. It was kind of like what they were doing to us. We slowed down the game a bit. It showed how together we were. Coach Flan told us to slow the game down and play a different type of game. We couldn't push the ball as much now so we had to adjust. It took a lot for us to adjust because it is not our game; but once we did it, we were able to break down the defense and see what they were doing and we were able to take command. They had commanded before that."

The Eagles held the ball for the first 2:09 of the overtime. Then, Walters' layup made it 54-52. Arlington would tie it at 54, but again the Bench Mob came through as Funderburk, who had made those three key free throws in the final two minutes of regulation, hit a pair of free throws to make it 56-54 with 58 seconds to play. The shots put the Eagles up for good.

"Mike Ryan had started for us all year (at center) and didn't even play in the overtime," Coach Bodle said. "That type of depth was phenomenal and we saw it. Usually to be a contender a team has to have decent kids and maybe six and seven. We could go to our ninth and 10th guy. To bring in a student-athlete like Andrew Dowell (a Division I college football prospect for 2015) as our 10th man, leaves a lot to be said for talent and depth. That's why we were able to weather some storms when kids got into foul trouble and a couple injuries."

Walters and Nichols would each score baskets and free throws in the final minute to make the difference. Nichols made 11 of 15 shots in the game and finished with a game-high 26 points. The final score read St. Ed's 62, Upper Arlington 58.

The Deuteronomy passage and the rest of the mind candy had played a big factor in this victory.

"When I see things like that in my players and I see that at practice, I know that when a situation comes up when we are trying to win a state championship game and we are down by six points with three minutes to go, I know they are looking at one another and saying, 'We are not going to lose,'" Coach Flannery said. "They see we are going to do whatever it takes, and they'll fight until the end. They were saying it out loud as we were coming into timeouts. When they buy into one another, they are going to fight until the end for one another. That's what made me so happy about this group winning it. They did it the right way. They did it themselves by taking ownership, and they did it because they wanted to win, not just for themselves but for one another."

Also playing a big factor had been the win against Ignatius the second time and the loss to Shaker a few days later because all three games were very similar, with the Eagles staging the kind of comebacks only champions can.

"The similarity in both games (Ignatius and Arlington) is that they realized it was late in the game and we had to do something," Coach Flannery concurred. "There is a sense of urgency that comes over them that they have to execute and play well. Even in the Shaker game we were down and said we have to make something. Sure enough, even though we lost that game, we had the ball with a chance to score to either tie it or win it. People could argue at the Arlington game that we had no business winning that game, being down by six with a minute and a half to go. It was late and we were down when that sense of urgency kicked in, and we had to pick it up at both ends of the floor. Fortunately we were good enough to execute it and pull out those games. Both in the Ignatius game and the Upper Arlington game, once we got it to overtime we felt like we won."

The difference between the '98 championship and this one was the journey.

"People have asked me – '98 or this year?" Flannery said. "The '98 win was special because it had been the first. We had done what we were supposed to do. This journey (in '14) because it was a lot longer of a wait – I appreciate it much more. I am not going to talk at all about which team was better. This journey I enjoyed a lot more."

Hamilton's performance at the end of regulation will be something no one who watched the game will forget, but the Eagles had several players who could have taken that shot.

"There was a reason why he (Hamilton) wasn't taking those shots (threes during the season)," Flannery said. "We would have a story if any one of the guys on the floor hit that shot, really. Kipper had an unbelievable final four. He was instrumental in our tournament run. It was appropriate for the best player at the time to hit down the shot. If Malcolm hit it, here's the two-guard who became the one-guard and he hits the big three -- the sacrifice that he made – that would have been a great story. If Tony hit it, there's our shooter, but he's also tough and our leader. If Derek or Mike Ryan made it, we would have thought that was crazy.

"The story with Marsalis is that here is a guy who is a four-year varsity player who went through a lot. He had that disappointment of getting to Columbus and not winning with his brother in 2012."

Then in 2012-13 Hamilton battled some injuries at the end of the year. He had a fracture in his back, which was why he didn't play well down the stretch. He was getting recruited at the Division I level then, and because of his injury he lost a lot of that.

"This year he could have come in and could have been very selfish like, 'I'm going to get mine; I need to get a scholarship,'" Coach Flannery said. "Yet, he sacrificed shooting threes and shooting jump shots and did what we asked him to do. We basically said that if we want to be good, he can't just sit there and shoot jump shots and threes. He had to attack the basket. He did that all year. After his good regional and sub-par final four, his coming full circle when we needed for him to hit a three-point shot to win or extend the state championship game was prodigious and rewarding."

Hamilton, who had played varsity since his freshman year, was happy to get that moment for himself and his teammates in a very unselfish moment that made him the hero.

"When we were down by six, I told my team we were going to win this game," Hamilton said. "We had worked too hard to just fall right now. I felt comfortable with taking the shot. Coach Flan gets on me sometimes for taking threes, but sometimes I have to do it. The key is to just take it with confidence."

Funderburk had played a big role in the championship game, particularly with his free-throw shooting and assist in the final two minutes of regulation.

"The Shaker game is the best game of the year. D.J. doesn't play. We don't play well, and we come back with the ball twice in the last minute after being down 11 with two minutes to go with a chance to tie it or take the lead," Coach Nugent said. "Coach (Flannery) said it that it was the moment when we said we could be pretty special. They just kept coming and kept coming and kept coming. We almost stole it from them in the end. Doesn't that show up a month later in the state championship game? (Funderburk's playing and contributing in the final seconds of regulation and the team's great comeback in the end) The way a team like Upper Arlington played, we go down six with two and a half minutes to play. We were like, uh, oh. They could control the ball. The doubt starts to creep in except on that bench. Those guys have been in that kind of situation before; they believed, they never stopped fighting, they kept going. This time it worked out. We had failed early in the year and succeeded later when it mattered most."

The Eagles shot 61 percent from the field and 71 percent from the line.

"I couldn't ask for a better performance from our guys," Coach Flannery said. "I look at our statistics that Coach (Tim) Smith does – that game was the most efficient in the last 20 years of state championship game statistics, and that's as far back as we could go. St. Edward was the most highly efficient team for a championship game in the last 20 years. The second most efficient team in the last 20 years was Upper Arlington. We played the most efficient basketball game on record for the last 20 years. It could be a lot more than that."

Vuyancih recalled coming to a state tournament as a young child and cherished the moment after the game while reflecting on the win.

"The first time I ever came to a state basketball tournament was when I was a kid and came to watch St. Ed's," said Vuyancih. "Growing up, all I ever wanted was to win a state championship for St. Edward, which is a great community. I love them so much. We trusted Marsalis to shoot the ball. I saw him hit that shot over and over again in practice. I knew it would be good."

Through urgency, next-play, earning/learning, collective responsibility, divine inspiration, Big Mike, bonding, the Bench Mob, ownership, mind-candy and toughness, the 2013-14 Eagles had proven they were truly Worthy of the Jersey.

Epilogue

Worthy of the Next Play, Continuing the Tradition

One hopes that success will breed success. Because these 18 student-athletes were part of a state championship, one hopes they would continue to be successful.

"Individually, you never know," Coach Flannery said. "People make mistakes; people go their own paths. As a group, they now have that aura about them of being successful. That breeds success down the line with confidence."

"I've seen it the other way, too. Some guys who have had a lot of success rely too much on that success -- their basketball success – and don't listen to the message about going to school and how important it is. There are some guys who have always been patted on the back and told how great they were. Things probably came easy for them on the basketball court that they slacked in other areas. Maybe they didn't focus as much on school, and maybe they got away with doing some things off the court because they were good basketball players. It could hurt them in a lot of decisions they make because they weren't held accountable for some of their actions. I see guys 15 years later and more mature, and they really see their mistakes and their successes. They have learned from all of them."

In college and in their future work lives, these student-athletes will be asked to be parts of teams. Their roles on a championship team could come into play.

"It could be impressive to an employer who asks what his role was on the team and then a Connor Pisco talks about his role on the team,"

Coach Nugent said. "That goes a long way. It's valuable. It's why sports are so important in life. There's people on the other side who say there's too much importance and too much money (placed into sports), but youth sports is where we are learning these lessons and the kind of teamwork it takes to accomplish great things outside the sport arena. I believe wholeheartedly that there are guys who can put on their resumes, 'I was part of a state championship team. I know what it takes to be part of a great team.'"

At minimum, a championship instills confidence in the players to succeed in other parts of life as adults.

"The successes on the court lead to successes off the court," Pisco said. "What we learned during the season is that through hard work and dedication, we can accomplish anything we want. It's something Coach Flan and all the coaches instilled into us."

Hamilton will play on scholarship at Division II Ashland; Vuyancih will play with his brother at Division III John Carroll; and, Walters will be a preferred walk-on at Division I Akron. Riley, Meyer, and Jack Flannery attend Ohio State but are not playing. "Every time I walk by Value City Arena going to a class or something, I'll remember the state championship." Riley said.

Other seniors include Justin Follmer, who is at Cleveland State; Connor Pisco, who is at Dayton; and Phil Parente, who is at the University of Cincinnati. None of the three will play college basketball.

Flannery has been part of eight teams that have made it to the final four. Of those eight, three have made it to the title game and two have won. However, that's still getting very close eight times in fewer than 20 years.

"To get there we have to win five straight games against tough competition," Coach Flannery said. "Then when we get there, we're at a different venue with a bigger crowd. Not everybody responds the same. We are playing against teams that are all confident, very excited, and playing their best basketball. They are there for a reason. It all comes down to how we match up. In '97 we went and we lost to Zanesville, the No. 1 ranked team in the state and undefeated. People thought that it was an upset, but they had two guys who went on to play in the NBA.

"In 2007 we had what I thought was one of our best teams, and we lost to Moeller, which was playing well. They had a tough style to play against. We had the experience against East Tech. We had a team that was more on a mission. We were more focused and thought that we were a little better than they were. We had a couple guys who had played on the final-four team in 2012. We were a little bit more driven. What's the difference between us losing to Newark in 2008 and 2014? Newark just played very well that night and we did not."

Flannery strongly believes that the more a program is in the final four, the more comfortable the coaches and players are.

"I feel more comfortable when we get there," Coach Flannery said. "I don't know if my message is any different. I say, 'You are going to enjoy this for the rest of your lives. Do you want to be remembered as a state final-four team or a state runner up or a state champ?' Now it goes back to the guys on the team. Are they listening and buying into the philosophy of earning everything and coaching one another through this? For us, Vuyancih was that guy. He had a team meeting the night before we went down there and called all the guys into his room. I don't know what was said in that meeting. That message coming from within is bigger than any message that I could send."

Coaching can be overrated because the talent takes over on the floor, and because the players need to take over. They are talking on the floor and being the voice.

"They have to trust one another," Coach Flannery explained. "I could talk until I am blue in the face, but are we going to win? A simpler and consistent message is best. I've learned to peal back."

Flannery tells his players he is never going to make the shot or miss the shot or play defense. He is showing them or telling them what they have to do, but it's up to them to do it.

"It's up to them to execute," Coach Flannery said. "Imagine teenagers. They want to hear that this is it and go. They don't want to be standing around in practice. They want to be playing. The same message is sent to everybody. They don't need to hear every detail. They just need to get guidance and structure and know where they are going. If the young man is not doing it right, I don't change. I keep telling him what he is supposed to do until he gets it. The same message is sent off the floor."

Coaching does play a part in winning championships, but Coach Flannery gives more credit to the kind of student-athletes he has had: their talent, their buying into earning their keeps, taking ownership, playing unselfishly, taking collective responsibility and accountability and being tough mentally.

"I know I am the head coach and ultimately the responsibility falls on me, good or bad," Coach Flannery said. "We try to admit when things do go well that it is the kids. They're the center and they're the reason for success because of their talent."

As a coach he spends a lot of time emphasizing his philosophy to his team, both on and off the court.

"We as a staff this year made sure they didn't get away with anything and as coaches we did a good job of focusing the next-play mentality," he said. "If the coaches see me get rattled on the sidelines, or I get rattled in the huddle, then they get rattled. Down to the championship game, I was constantly building confidence in them that they were going to win. I wanted them to put plenty of time into living the moment and focus on what we do next."

He has done a pretty good job of keeping his cool and remaining calm. Over the years, one of the keys to his success has been his ability to keep things in perspective. It goes back to his formative years at St. Ed's.

"I always take it from when I played," Coach Flannery said. "What I mean is I remember when I played, I missed shots. I turned the ball over. I had days when I didn't play hard and didn't want to be there even though they were few. I remember what it was like to be a player and I was not perfect. If they are giving me their all, there is not much I can ask from my guys other than to play smart, and to do what we are telling them to do, or at least *try* to do what we are telling them to do."

While he has learned much from USA Basketball, from the coaches he has served under for many years as an assistant at St. Ed's, and from his current assistants, Flannery has become his own coach. He does things his own way, which has led to much of this success at St. Ed's.

"After this year I am more of a believer now that I can actually teach kids to be leaders," Coach Flannery said. "It can be done. People say leaders are born, and there is some truth to that. Someone needs to have a certain personality to be a true leader. I think some of these guys have learned over the last year and half to become leaders. Guys stepped up to their roles and stepped out of their comfort zone probably more than any other group of guys I have had."

Another aspect to coaching is preparing his student-athletes to extend their playing careers.

Flannery tells the youth and parents that one of his responsibilities is to help them get into college, and that if they want to play college basketball they have the opportunity to do so.

"If someone makes it through four years from his freshman year when there are 65 players who want to play basketball, it means he has made it further than nearly 60 others," Coach Flannery said. "I never promise where they are going to play or at what level they are going to play. I can't make a kid something he is not. However, if someone makes it through a program like ours, he should be able to play at some level. Jake Lorbach at Ohio State walked on and made the team."

Coaches Bodle and Flannery have talked about the next play, and how it is not about yesterday or tomorrow but about today – the present. Few teams have been able to win back-to-back state championships in Ohio, but that is no reason not to have that goal.

"Right after we get the first one and get a taste of that blood, we want to get it again. It's not easy, but I think we could do it," said Nichols, who will be a senior on the 2014-15 team. "We know what it takes."

Things could get even better.

"When we talk about next season, I had thought at the beginning of this season (2013-14) that it could be special, but I thought that next year we could be as good as or better," Coach Flannery said. "I still believe that. We have guys who are experienced now, who know what it takes. If they build upon that, we could be just as good or better. We have a lot of work to do if we want to do it again. This was fun. I loved this. This is as good as it gets. I will enjoy it for forever. I want to do it again, and I don't want to wait 16 years again."

Every team goes through some struggles every year. As a team, they have to overcome that.

"It could be something in the classroom that they are trying to fight through," Coach Flannery said. "They have to show up every day at practice, and they still have to fight through that stuff. They have to keep that focus of playing basketball as one of their priorities. It's not always easy to do. Overcoming those things just adds to the drama or euphoria of winning the state championship. Some days these kids are here until 8 o'clock at night. They get here at 6 in the morning."

It starts at the end of the previous season. They have to get better as a team and they have to get better as coaches. They have to send that message right away that they are committed to doing that. It will be a matter of finding new leaders.

"They were holding one another accountable," Coach Flannery said. "'Why aren't you here today?' they ask. I tell the guys, 'Don't come to me if your teammates aren't showing up.' I'm just going to cut them when the time comes. If you want to win and you think they are important to the team, then you get on them. That is your teammate and that is how we are going to win it. If you don't care, that means you are selfish. A selfish player would say, 'He's a good player and he is not showing up; then good, I am just going to get more points and I am just going to get more publicity.' If he really cares about winning, then he is going to do his best to get everybody to show up and do the same things that he is doing."

Preparing never stops. As this book was being finished, Coach Flannery was returning from Dubai, coaching the USA U-17 team to a world championship and a gold medal. The students were heading back to school, and the team was already in the weight room and the gym preparing for the defense of their title.

Such is the story of a team that *learned* and then *earned* a state championship and, in the process, became worthy of their jerseys.

Bibliography

Krzyzewski, Mike, and Donald T. Phillips. *Five-Point Play: Duke's Journey to the 2001 National Championship.* Warner Books, 2001.

Bilas, Jay. *Toughness: Developing True Strength On And Off The Court.* New American Library, 2013.